<u>*Introduction*</u>

This book provides concise coverage of the Key Stage Four syllabus
for <u>*GCSE French*</u> up to Higher Level with particular emphasis on
essential Grammar. It offers a comprehensive reference section
including both French-English and English-French dictionaries.

Our Guides have <u>*three features*</u> which set them apart from the rest:

Careful and Concise Explanations

We work hard to give everything you need to know for
each topic, but without including any unecessary waffle.

Deliberate Use of Humour and Relaxed English

We consider the humour to be an essential part of our Revision
Guides. It is there to keep the reader interested and entertained, and
we are certain that it greatly assists their learning. It is not however
expected to win us any awards...

Constant Emphasis on Learning the Basic Facts

All our Guides underline the inescapable need to keep learning the
basic facts. This simple message is hammered home without
compromise and without remorse, and whilst this traditionally brutal
philosophy may not be quite in line with some other approaches to
education, we still rather like it. But only because it works.

Contents

Essential Grammar

The World Around You

The Wider World

Exams and Reference

Published by Coordination Group Publications
Typesetting and layout by The French Coordination Group
Original illustrations by: Sandy Gardner, e-mail: illustrations@sandygardner.co.uk

Co-edited by Simon Cook BA (Hons)
Design Editor: James Paul Wallis BEng (Hons)

Contributors:
Angela Blacklock-Brown
Alistair Campbell
Alan Dent
Sarah Donachie
Colette Patten

Text, design, layout and illustrations © Richard Parsons 1998, 1999
All rights reserved.

ISBN   1-84146-801-0

Groovy website: www.cgpbooks.co.uk

With thanks to Steve Brain and Angela Blacklock-Brown for the proof-reading.
Jolly bits of clipart from CorelDRAW

Printed by Elanders Hindson, Newcastle upon Tyne.

0999

Nouns

The biggest difference between French and English is that the French language has *'gender'* — this means every <u>noun</u> is either <u>masculine</u> or <u>feminine</u>. And that makes French pretty complicated.

A Noun is a Person, Place, Thing or Animal

For example : <u>cat</u>, <u>house</u>, <u>table</u>, <u>mother</u>. Names of <u>people</u> and <u>places</u> are also nouns.

1) Every noun in French is either <u>masculine</u> or <u>feminine</u>.
2) Every noun must have an <u>article</u> in front of it — eg: <u>un</u>, <u>une</u>, <u>des</u>. This article tells you exactly what <u>gender</u> (masculine or feminine) and <u>number</u> (singular or plural) of the noun is.

You've got to remember to use the masculine, feminine or plural form of the article.

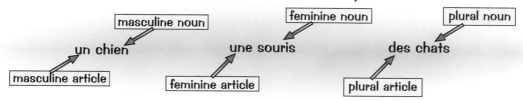

masculine noun → un chien ← masculine article

feminine noun → une souris ← feminine article

plural noun → des chats ← plural article

There are 3 different types of articles and it's <u>really important</u> you get them all learned. The one above is called the <u>indefinite article</u> — but you just need to know that it means '<u>a</u>' or '<u>an</u>'.

> Use <u>un</u> for <u>masculine singular</u> nouns
> Use <u>une</u> for <u>feminine singular</u> nouns
> Use <u>des</u> for <u>plural</u> nouns

Making Nouns Plural

1) Nouns in French are usually made plural by adding an '<u>s</u>' — just like English really.

 eg: une orange → des orange<u>s</u>
orange → oranges

2) But there are always <u>exceptions</u> to the rule in French. The nouns in the table below have a <u>different</u> plural form — and this lot are just the beginning.

Noun ending	Irregular plural ending	Example
-ail	-aux	travail → travaux
-al	-aux	journal → journaux
-eau	-eaux	bureau → bureaux
-eu	-eux	jeu → jeux
-ou	-oux	chou → choux

un oeil   trois yeux

You'll have to learn these nouns by practising over and over. Some nouns have completely <u>irregular</u> plurals, eg: <u>oeil</u> → <u>yeux</u> (eye → eyes).

3) Some nouns <u>don't change</u> in the plural. These are usually nouns that end in <u>-s</u>, <u>-x</u> or <u>-z</u>.

 un nez → des nez   a nose → noses
un os → des os   a bone → bones

4) <u>The key point</u> to remember is if you're going to make the <u>noun</u> plural, then <u>always</u> make the <u>article</u> that goes with it <u>plural</u> too — if they go together then they should <u>agree</u>.

The Gender problem — the battle of the sexists...

This sounds a bit confusing, but once you've got your head round it it won't seem half as bad. The thing to do is to make sure that <u>every time</u> you learn a new <u>noun</u>, you also learn whether it's <u>masculine</u> or <u>feminine</u>, and what its <u>plural</u> is. You can get all this from a French dictionary.

2

Adjectives

An _adjective_ is a word which _describes_ a noun. Sounds easy enough, but don't forget that in French you've got to match up the _gender_ — a bit like a blind date really.

Adjectives _must 'Agree' with the Noun_

1) French adjectives can have up to four different forms — _masculine singular_, _feminine singular_, _masculine plural_ and _feminine plural_.
2) 'Agree' means the adjective has to have the _same gender_ and _number_ as the noun it describes ie. _agree_ with it. If the adjective describes a _feminine noun_, it must be in its _feminine form_ etc.
3) The form of any adjective you find in the _dictionary_ is the _masculine singular_ form. Don't ask me why — it must have been a load of blokes who wrote the dictionary.

1) _Making adjectives Feminine — adding an 'e'_

1) To make an adjective feminine you usually just add an _e_ to the masculine singular form.
eg: grand → grand_e_   big   petit → petit_e_   small
    vert → vert_e_   green   noir → noir_e_   black
2) If the masculine form of an adjective already ends in _-e_, it _doesn't_ change.

2) _Making adjectives Plural_

Plural adjectives are very similar to nouns:
1) Most _masculine adjectives_ add '_s_' to form the plural.
2) _Feminine adjectives_ add an '_s_' to become plural.

But hey — it'd be much too easy if that was all there was to it.
Adjectives ending in _-x_, _-f_, _-er_, _-on_, _-en_, _-el_ and _-il_ follow different rules:

Il est sportif

Elle est sportive

Adjective ending	Example	masculine singular	feminine singular	masculine plural	feminine plural
-x	heureux (also sérieux, curieux, ennuyeux, délicieux, dangereux, merveilleux)	heureux	heureuse	heureux	heureuses
-f	actif (also vif, sportif)	actif	active	actifs	actives
-er	premier (also dernier, fier, cher, étranger)	premier	première	premiers	premières
-on, -en, -el, -il	bon (also mignon, ancien, parisien, cruel, gentil)	bon	bonne	bons	bonnes

And there are also some adjectives which are _completely irregular_ — you're just going to have to learn these ones off by heart. So get started right now.

masculine singular	before a m sglr noun beginning with a vowel or an h	feminine singular	masculine plural	feminine plural
vieux	vieil	vieille	vieux	vieilles
beau	bel	belle	beaux	belles
nouveau	nouvel	nouvelle	nouveaux	nouvelles
fou	fol	folle	fous	folles
long	—	longue	longs	longues
blanc	—	blanche	blancs	blanches
tout	—	toute	tous	toutes

Position _of Adjectives_

1) In French _most_ adjectives _follow_ the noun.

eg:

noun ↘
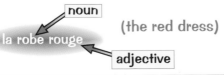
la robe rouge   (the red dress)
↖ adjective

2) But some common adjectives come _before_ the noun — a real pain. They're listed below.

grand, gros, petit, long, bon, mauvais, beau, meilleur, nouveau, vieux, joli, jeune

More Adjectives

Adjectives can Change Meaning depending on Position

Some adjectives *change their meaning* according to whether they are *before* or *after* the noun. It's dead important you learn these *carefully*.

adjective	meaning if before noun	meaning if after noun	Example
ancien	former	old/ancient	un ancien soldat (a former soldier)
			une maison ancienne (an old house)
cher	dear	expensive	mon cher ami (my dear friend)
			une voiture chère (an expensive car)
propre	own	clean	ma propre chambre (my own room)
			ma chambre est propre (my room is clean)
grand	great	tall	un grand ami (a great friend)
			un homme grand (a tall man)
pauvre	poor (deserves sympathy)	poor (short of money)	le pauvre homme (the poor man)
			l'homme pauvre (the poor man)

Possessive Adjectives — how to say My, His, Your...

When you want to say that something *belongs* to a person, you need to use the *possessive adjectives* listed below. They each have three forms, *masculine singular*, *feminine singular* and *plural*.

Remember — the form you use depends on the *gender* and *number* of the *noun* the adjective refers to, *NOT* the owner of the noun.

Before a noun beginning with a *vowel* or an '*h*' always use the masculine form.

	masculine singular	feminine singular	plural
my	mon	ma	mes
your	ton	ta	tes
his/her/its	son	sa	ses
our	notre	notre	nos
your	votre	votre	vos
their	leur	leur	leurs

The form of these adjectives depends on the noun described *not* the person who owns it — so even though *son* is a masculine form it can mean *his*, *hers* or *its*; and so can sa and ses.

Indefinite Adjectives — some Really Useful words

Here are some words you can't do without — they'll help your French writing get you loads of marks:

eg: *Chaque* homme a le *même* chien.
Each man has the same dog

They all go *before* the noun!

autre	*other*
chaque	*each*
même	*same*
plusieurs	*several*
quelque(s)	*some*
tout, toute, tous, toutes	*all*
tel, telle, tels, telles	*such*

Demonstrative Adjectives — This, That, These, Those

masculine singular	masculine singular before vowel or silent h	feminine singular	plural
ce	cet	cette	ces

ce stylo *this pen*	cet oiseau *this bird*
cette maison *this house*	ces pommes *these apples*

Stick *-ci* or *-là* to the noun to mean 'this ... here' or 'that ... there':

ce stylo-ci *this pen here*　cette maison-là *that house there*　ces pommes-ci *these apples here*

Adjectives should agree — no they shouldn't...

Making adjectives *agree* seems tricky, but with *practice* you'll get used to it. Some have different meanings depending on whether they're *before* or *after* the noun — so be careful here.

Using Adjectives

You need Adjectives to describe things

To describe things you use an _adjective_ — don't forget that the adjective _changes_ according to _gender_ (masculine or feminine) and _number_ (singular or plural).

The RULE is:-

adjective as found in dictionary	_masculine singular_
adjective + _e_ (if no e already)	_feminine singular_
adjective + _s_	_masculine plural_
adjective + _es_	_feminine plural_

Here are some examples to illustrate the rules:

_le_ pantalon est _bleu_   the trousers are blue
_la_ chemise est _bleue_   the shirt is blue

les chapeaux sont _verts_   the hats are green
les jupes sont _vertes_   the skirts are green

The Three Big Problems that Adjectives can cause you

> 1) Their _position_ (before or after the noun)
> 2) _Spelling changes_ for the feminine form
> 3) Their _meaning_ before or after the noun

1) a) _Colours and nationalities come after the noun._

une maison rouge   a red house
_un_ drapeau français   a French flag

b) _This group of adjectives comes before the noun:_

jeune	_young_	joli	_nice_	petit	_small_
grand	_big_	pauvre	_poor_	court	_short_
long(ue)	_long_	haut	_high_	gros(se)	_fat_
méchant	_naughty_	vilain	_ugly_	mauvais	_bad_

c) _These adjectives are irregular — you're really going to need to learn them I'm afraid._

m sglr	m word beginning with a vowel/silent h	m plural	f sglr	f plural	English
beau	bel	beaux	belle	belles	beautiful
nouveau	nouvel	nouveaux	nouvelle	nouvelles	new
vieux	vieil	vieux	vieille	vieilles	old

2) a) _Certain adjectives have a consonant change before the feminine ending._

| blanc blan**che** _white_ | franc fran**che** _frank_ | sec sè**che** _dry_ |
| vif vi**ve** _lively_ | neuf neu**ve** _new_ | |

b) _Some adjectives double the consonant before adding the feminine ending._

bon bon**ne** _good_   ancien ancien**ne** _old_   gros gros**se** _fat_

3) _Some adjectives change their meaning according to their position (see P.3)._

| un livre cher | an _expensive_ book | une chère amie | a _dear_ friend |
| une chemise propre | a _clean_ shirt | ma propre chambre | my _own_ room |

Cher — an expensive old dear...

All the little quirks and difficulties of adjectives. It looks like a bit of a nightmare, I know, but take it _bit by bit_ and you'll get there.

Articles — "A", "The" and "Some"

Articles sound pretty tough but really they're just the wee words that go _in front_ of _nouns_ — telling you if a noun's _masculine_, _feminine_ or _plural_. There are _3_ kinds: _Indefinite_, _Definite_ and _Partitive_.

The Indefinite Article means 'a' or 'an'

You've met this article already (P.1), but learn the note:

m sglr	f sglr	m and f plural
un	une	des

Note: the indefinite article is left out when you're talking about people's occupations.
eg: Il est professeur   _He is a teacher_

Le, la and les mean 'the' — using the Definite Article

m sglr	f sglr	before a vowel	m and f plural
le	la	l'	les

1) If you want to translate English '_the_', you'll need _le_, _la_, _l'_ or _les_ in French.

2) However, this article is used _loads more_ in French than 'the' is used in English.

eg: _Les_ chats détestent _les_ araignées   _Cats hate spiders_   J'aime _le_ football   _I like football_

3) The prepositions '_à_' or '_de_' (see P.8) _combine_ with the definite article as shown opposite.

	m sglr	f sglr	before a vowel	m and f plural
à	au	à la	à l'	aux
de	du	de la	de l'	des

How to say 'some' or 'any' — the Partitive Article

If you say "_some_ bread" or ask "have you got _any_ bread?" you are using the _partitive article_.

m sglr	f sglr	before a vowel	m and f plural
du	de la	de l'	des

eg: _Avez-vous du pain?_   _Have you got any bread?_
    Il a de l'argent   _He has some money_

KEY POINT — This article is just like _le_, _la_, and _les_ combined with '_de_'. So when you're reading or listening to French you've got to be very careful to pay attention to the _context_ to work out _which one_ is being used. If you're careless you'll only be throwing important marks away.

Three More Mega-Important Points

1) After a Negative (_ne .... pas_) the partitive article shrinks to _de_ (_d'_ before a _vowel_ or an _h_)
eg: J'ai _des_ copains français   _I have some French friends_ →   Je n'ai pas _de_ copains français

2) Before an Adjective coming in front of a noun, the partitive article again shrinks to _de_ or _d'_.
eg: _des_ maisons _some houses_   →   _de_ grandes maisons   _some big houses_

3) After expressions of Quantity only _de_ or _d'_ are used:

assez	enough		peu	little, a few
beaucoup	much, a lot of		plus	more
combien?	how much?		trop	too much, too many
moins	less			

Beaucoup de frites!

A load of articles — sounds like a boring newspaper...

Definite, Indefinite and Partitive look confusing, but they're just the "_an_", "_the_" and "_some_" words that go with nouns. Don't forget, you need the _correct form_ of the article to go with the _noun_.

Adverbs

Adverbs describe *how* something is done, or an action is performed, eg: *quietly*, *loudly*, *quickly*.
Adverbs do **NOT** have to *agree* with anything, so they are a lot less complicated than adjectives

Using Adverbs to describe Verbs

1) Most adverbs are formed by adding *-ment* to the *feminine* form of the adjective.
     eg: tendre → tendre*ment*   tender → tenderly
           clair → claire → claire*ment*   clear → clearly

2) Of course there are *exceptions* to this rule. Some of the most important ones are below:-

énormément	=	enormously
souvent	=	often
gentiment	=	nicely
vraiment	=	really, truly
vite	=	quickly
évidemment	=	evidently
trop	=	too
assez	=	fairly
si	=	so

J'ai si faim!
Je pourrais avaler
un boeuf!

Ah! Un bon
repas, j'ai bien
mangé!

3) The adverb equivalents of *bon* (good) and *mauvais*
(bad) are *'bien'* and *'mal'*. Make sure that you use
bien and mal to describe *verbs* and bon and
mauvais to describe *nouns*. *DON'T mix them up*

4) Adverbs usually go *after* the verb.
     eg: *Je peux nager vite*   I can swim quickly
           Il est vraiment gentil   He is really nice

5) If you're using the perfect tense (see P.18) the adverb goes *between* the bit of avoir or être
and the past participle (although there are a few exceptions to this — you'll learn by practice).
     eg: *Il a bien nagé*   He swam well

Interrogative Adverbs are used to Ask Questions

Combien?	*How much?*
Comment?	*How?*
Où?	*Where?*
Pourquoi?	*Why?*
Quand?	*When?*

J'ai trop mangé

Quand est-ce que tu pars?   *When are you leaving?*
Où est la poste?   *Where is the post office?*
Ça fait *combien*?   *How much is that?*
Tu viens? *Pourquoi* pas?   *Are you coming? Why not?*
Comment t'appelles-tu?   *What are you called? — literally 'How do you call yourself?'*

It ain't what you do — it's the way that you do it...

Adverbs describe *actions* and *adjectives* describe *people* and *things* — don't forget the difference
between bien/mal and bon/mauvais. The great thing here is that adverbs don't have to agree
with anything. Remember, "interrogative adverbs" is just a posh name for question words.

Comparatives and Superlatives

To get top marks in the Exam you need to be able to _compare things_ and say which is _better_ or _best_ — and you've got to use your _adjectives_ and _adverbs_ for that. So get them learned now.

Comparatives — _how to compare things_

Comparing People or Things = plus, moins, aussi + adjective + que

Comparing Actions = plus, moins, aussi + adverb + que

1) To say "_more than_" you must use "_plus... ...que_".
2) To say "_less than_" you must use "_moins... ...que_".
3) To say "_as much as/the same as_" you must use "_aussi... ...que_".
4) The "_plus_", "_moins_" or "_aussi_" always goes _before_ the adjective or adverb.

noun — more — adjective — as/than

Dougal est plus grand que Pierre
(Dougal is taller (more tall) than Pierre)

Pierre est moins grand que Dougal
(Pierre is not as tall (less tall) as Dougal)

Franz est aussi grand que Pierre
(Franz is as tall as Pierre)

Superlatives — _the most, the least, the best, etc._

Superlative of People or Things = le, la, les + plus/moins + adjective

Superlative of Actions = le + plus/moins + adverb

1) Remember that adjectives _agree_ with the noun.
2) By contrast, adverbs _never change_ — and with the superlative you _always_ use _le_ — and _never_ la or les:
   eg: "_Edith chante le plus fort_"
   Edith sings the loudest
3) You can also use the superlative to compare things _in_ a particular _group_. For that you need to use _de_ :
   eg: "_La fille la plus laide de l'école_"
   The ugliest girl in the school

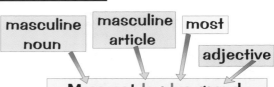

masculine noun — masculine article — most — adjective

Marc est le plus grand.
(Marc is the tallest (most tall))

Monique is a feminine noun

feminine article — adjective — Extra e because adjective must agree with Monique

Monique est la plus petite.

The Top Six Irregular Comparatives _and_ Superlatives

Comparatives	Superlatives
better (adjective) = _meilleur_	the best (adjective) = _le/la meilleur(e)_
worse (adjective) = _pire_	the worst (adjective) = _le/la pire_
better (adverb) = _mieux_	the best (adverb) = _le mieux_

Superlatively exciting — comparatively speaking...

Now you've hit the dizzy heights of saying that one thing is taller or better than another.
Remember _where_ the plus or moins goes, and that you always use _le_ with an _adverb_.

<u>Prepositions</u>

Prepositions are dead important — they're the words that make the sentence hang together.

<u>Prepositions are</u> *Linking Words*

They go *before nouns* and *link* them to the rest of the sentence. Start by learning the main ones:

à	*at, to, many different meanings*		en	*in, into*
après	*after*		entre	*between*
avant	*before (of time)*		jusqu'à	*until*
avec	*with*		malgré	*in spite of*
chez	*at the house of*		par	*by, through*
contre	*against*		parmi	*among*
dans	*in, into*		pendant	*during*
de	*of, from*		pour	*for*
déjà	*already*		sans	*without*
depuis	*since*		sauf	*except*
derrière	*behind*		sous	*under*
devant	*before (of place), in front of*		sur	*on, upon*

<u>KEY POINT</u> — French prepositions are NOT the same as English ones — eg: English *'in'* can be translated by several *different prepositions* which each possess *part* of the English meaning.

1) <u>English 'in' could be</u> en, dans <u>or</u> à

1) *'In'* is usually translated by *'en'* or *'dans'*.
   eg: <u>en</u> bonne santé   *in good health*
      Il y a une araignée <u>dans</u> ma chambre *There's a spider in my bedroom*

2) *'In'* (and *'at'* and *'to'*) with towns is always *'à'*.
        eg: j'habite <u>à</u> Paris   *I live in Paris*

3) To say *'in'* a country:

masculine singular countries = <u>à</u> + <u>definite article</u>	eg: <u>au</u> Portugal	*in Portugal*
feminine singular countries = <u>en</u>	eg: <u>en</u> France	*in France*
plural countries = <u>à</u> + <u>definite article</u>	eg: <u>aux</u> Pays-Bas	*in Holland*

2) <u>You can translate 'on' with</u> sur, à <u>or</u> en

'Sur' is used when *'on'* refers to something's *position* — eg: on top. But there are many other ways of translating 'on' in French as well, depending on when you're using it.

Moi!!

Sur la chaise   En vacances

<u>sur</u> la chaise	*on the chair*
<u>à</u> pied	*on foot*
<u>en</u> vacances	*on holiday*

<u>N.B.</u> If you want to say 'on Monday', 'on Tuesday' etc, you <u>don't</u> need to use a preposition in French: *Si on allait à la piscine <u>jeudi</u>?*
Shall we go to the swimming pool <u>on Thursday</u>?

3) <u>Translating 'about'</u> — what are you saying...

1) If 'about' means *'approximately'*, use *'à peu près'*.
  eg: J'ai <u>à peu près</u> vingt chaussettes   *I've got about 20 socks*
2) If 'about' means *'on the subject of'*, use *'au sujet de'* or *'à propos de'*.
  eg: Le film était <u>au sujet de</u> la guerre   *The film was about the war*
3) *'Environ'* means 'about' in the sense of *'around about'*.
  eg: Il était <u>environ</u> quatre heures   *It was about 4 o'clock*

Prepositions and Conjunctions

4) Depuis can mean 'since' or 'for'

Depuis translates as '_since_' or '_for_' (as in 'for a period of time'). If you use 'depuis' you must be really careful about the _tense_ of the verb you use with it.

1) If you want to say that you _have been_ doing something for a certain amount of time, and are _still doing it_, you must use the _present tense_ with depuis (see P.14).

   eg: *J'apprends l'allemand depuis trois mois*
        I have been learning German for 3 months

2) If you want to say that you _had been_ doing something, but you _don't do it anymore_, you must use the _imperfect tense_ with depuis (see P.20).

   eg: *Elle était végétarienne depuis trois ans, mais la semaine dernière elle a mangé un hamburger.*
       She had been vegetarian for three years, but last week she ate a hamburger

Conjunctions — words for joining and explaining

Conjunctions are like glue — they're the little words that stick all the different parts of a sentence together. Make sure you can _spell them_ all properly, and use them with the _right tenses_.

et	and
mais	but
donc	so, therefore
comme	as
si	if
que	that
quand	when

NOTE — This is totally different to _où_ (with an accent) meaning '_where_'

ou	or
ni	nor
pendant que	while, during
puisque	as, since, seeing that
tandis que	while, whilst
car	because
parce que	because

REMEMBER that this is _two_ words

Some Smashing Examples:

Je n'aime pas le français, <u>parce que</u> le professeur est ennuyeux.
I don't like French because the teacher is boring

Il a dit <u>qu'</u>il t'aime.
He said that he loves you

Ça doit être vrai, <u>puisque</u> le prof l'a dit.
It must be true, since the teacher said it

Je vais sortir ce soir, <u>tandis que</u> tu dois rester à la maison.
I'm going out this evening, while you have to stay at home

<u>Pendant qu'</u>elle regardait la télévision, il lisait son livre.
While she was watching television, he was reading his book

Je n'aime pas le français, parce que le professeur est ennuyeux!

Con-junction — a dodgy join...

These are all really useful — you couldn't make a sentence without them. Make sure you can recognise them and _use_ them. If you want to pick up top marks in the writing and speaking exams, sneak in a few phrases using _depuis_, or those conjunctions _puisque_ and _tandis que_.

Subject and Object Pronouns

Pronouns are substitute words — they _replace_ a _noun_ so you don't have to keep repeating it. Common ones are _I_, _me_, _she_, _it_ etc. Pronouns must be the same _gender_ and _number_ as the noun they replace.

The _Most Important Grammar Terms_ in the World...Ever

SUBJECT = the person/ thing who does the action
OBJECT = the thing that the action is performed on

| subject | | subject pronoun |

The boy liked the dog.   **He liked it.**

| verb | object | | object pronoun |

Subject _Pronouns Replace_ the _Subject_ of the Sentence

je	I	nous	we
tu	you (familiar)	vous	you (polite/plural)
il	he	ils	they (all masculine or mixed)
elle	she	elles	they (all female)
on	one	(NOTE: 'on' is used a lot in French and isn't posh)	

a) **TU and VOUS** — _Tu_ is used for speaking to _one person_, and only for _friends_, _relatives_ and _children_. _Vous_ is used instead of tu for talking to people you _don't know_ very well and people who are _older_ than you. It's also used for talking to _more than one person_.
b) **ILS and ELLES** — if 'they' refers to a _mixed group_ of masculines and feminines, use '_ils_'.

Object _Pronouns Replace_ the _Object_ of the Sentence

Object pronouns are used _instead of_ object nouns — you only need to learn _two kinds_:

1) _Direct Object_ **Pronouns are** _directly involved_ **in the action**

The French direct object pronouns are:

me	me	nous	us
te	you	vous	you
le	him/it	les	them
la	her/it		

me, te, le and la become m', t' and l' before a _vowel_

The boy liked the dog.
Le garçon a aimé le chien.

He liked it.
Il l'a aimé.

| subject | object | object pronoun |

Example:
- Qui aime les pommes?   _Who likes apples?_
- Je les aime   _I like them_

In the example above the dog is a _direct object_, so it's _replaced_ by a _direct object pronoun_.

How to get yourself some _Top Extra Marks_

This is a great way to get bonus marks — but make sure you know the perfect tense first (P.18)

HOT TIP: When the _direct object pronoun_ comes _before_ the _auxiliary verb_ in the perfect tense, then the _past participle_ has to _agree_ with the pronoun in _gender_ and _number_.

Example: Qui a mangé _les pommes_?   Je _les_ ai mang_és_.

_No_ agreement of past participle, as direct object _follows_ the verb.

Past participle adds _-es_ for feminine plural, as pommes is _feminine plural_ and the direct object pronoun '_les_' which replaces pommes comes _before_ the verb.

Object Pronouns and "En" and "Y"

2) Indirect Object Pronouns — 'to me', 'to you' etc.

The _indirect object_ is the person or thing _to_ whom or _for_ whom something is done.

| direct object | indirect object | indirect object pronoun |

I gave a present to John.　　I gave him a present.

If a sentence has an _indirect object_ it always has the preposition _à_ — but when the indirect object is _replaced_ by an _indirect object pronoun_ there's _no à_

The French _indirect object pronouns_ are:

me	to me	nous	to us
te	to you	vous	to you
lui	to him	leur	to them
lui	to her		

J'ai donné un cadeau _à John_ → Je _lui_ ai donné un cadeau

WATCH OUT — Some French verbs take an indirect object when their English equivalents do not. Some common verbs which do this are: demander _à_, téléphoner _à_, servir _à_.

Je vais téléphoner _à_ John et Marie ce soir　I'm going to phone John and Marie this evening
Je vais _leur_ téléphoner ce soir　　　　　　I'm going to phone them this evening

Two Top Words — 'En' & 'Y'

1) _EN_ — this pronoun translates as '_of it_', '_of them_', '_some_' or '_any_'.

eg: J'_en_ prends trois　_I'll have three of them_

If a verb is followed by _de_, '_it_' or '_them_' is translated by '_en_'.
eg: avoir besoin de　_to need_
J'_en_ ai besoin　_I need it_

2) _Y_ — this wee fella means '_there_'.
eg: J'_y_ vais　　_I'm going there_
It's used to mean '_it_' or '_them_' after verbs followed by _à_, eg: penser.
eg: Je n'_y_ pense plus
I don't think about it anymore
It's also used in several common expressions.
Il _y_ a　　there is/there are
Ça _y_ est!　that's it! - as in 'I've finished!'

Stick all Object Pronouns Before the Verb

Pronouns always go _before_ the verb. If you're using _two_ object pronouns in the same sentence, they _both_ go before the verb, but they go in a _special order_. This is a bit tricky so get it learned:

1	2	3	4	5	6
me te nous vous	le la les	lui leur	y	en	(verb)

Examples: Il _me les_ donne
He gives them to me
Je _le lui_ ai donné
I gave it to him

If you are using a _negative_, the '_ne_' goes _before_ the object pronoun, and the '_pas_' after the verb.
Example: Je ne _les_ mange pas　I don't eat them

I'll subject you to more of this — if you don't object...

Lots of confusing terminology, but what's actually going on _isn't_ that complicated. That's the thing with grammar, full of posh names for ordinary words that seem designed to put you off. Anyway, _learn_ your _pronouns_ and the _order_ that they go in. You'll find _en_ and _y_ rather useful.

More Pronouns

Emphatic Pronouns are used to emphasise things

An emphatic pronoun is a way of highlighting who was involved in the sentence.

moi	*I/me*	elle	*she/her*	eux	*them (m)*
toi	*you*	nous	*we/us*	elles	*them (f)*
lui	*he/him*	vous	*you*		

Emphatic pronouns are used:

1) To emphasise the person who has performed an action.
eg: <u>Lui</u>! Il ne le sait pas!   *Him! He doesn't know!*

2) After prepositions
eg: chez <u>moi</u>   *at my house*
      après <u>toi</u>   *after you*

3) In comparisons
eg: Il est plus intelligent que <u>moi</u>.
      He is more intelligent than me

4) In a command
eg: Écoutez-<u>moi</u>   *Listen to me*

5) They can stand alone, as an answer to a question for example.
eg: Qui a cassé la fenêtre? *Who broke the window?*
    <u>Lui</u>!   *Him!*

6) They can combine with même to mean myself, yourself, himself etc.
      <u>moi</u>-même   *myself*   <u>eux</u>-mêmes   *themselves*

Demonstrative Pronouns — this one, that one, these ones, those ones

These smashing pronouns are used for pointing things out.

m sglr	f sglr	m plural	f plural
celui	celle	ceux	celles

You can also add the endings <u>-ci</u> and <u>-là</u> to stress 'this one <u>here</u>' or 'that one <u>there</u>'.

eg: J'ai deux chiens. <u>Celui-ci</u> est mignon, mais <u>celui-là</u> est méchant.
    I've got two dogs. This one here's nice, but that one there's nasty

Mes chaussures sont bleues, mais <u>celles-là</u> sont vertes.
My shoes are blue, but those ones there are green

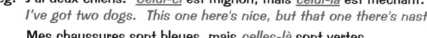

Two more demonstrative pronouns are:

ceci	=	this
cela	=	that — often shortened to 'ça'

eg: *Cela n'est pas vrai*   *That's not true*
     Lisez ceci   *Read this*

These are <u>INVARIABLE</u> — they <u>don't change</u> no matter what gender of noun they replace.

Several, some, a few... — they call 'em Indefinite Pronouns

There's nothing particularly special about these, you just need to be able to understand and use them:

quelque chose	*something*	plusieurs	*several*
quelqu'un	*somebody/someone*	chacun	*each one*
autre	*other, another*	certains	*some*
tout	*everything, all*	pas grand-chose	*nothing much*
quelques-uns	*some, a few*		

Relative and Interrogative Pronouns

Relative Pronouns — talking about people or things

Qui, Que and Dont

1) *Dont* means '*whose*' or '*of which*'. It always goes *before* the noun.

   eg: Ce livre, <u>dont</u> l'auteur est inconnu, est très intéressant

       This book, whose author is unknown, is very interesting

2) Both *qui* and *que* can mean *who*, *which* or *what*. The difficulty is knowing which one to use.

  a) *qui* — used to replace the *subject* of the sentence.

  eg: Elle est la fille <u>qui</u> a frappé le professeur   *She's the girl who hit the teacher*

  b) *que* — to replace the *object* of the sentence.

  eg: C'est la pire chose <u>que</u> j'ai faite *It's the worst thing that I've done*

    <u>BUT</u> — you <u>NEVER</u> use *que* after a *preposition*.

'The......which' — Lequel

Another set of relative pronouns are used after prepositions to refer to '*things*' (not people). They mean '*the ...... which*'.

m sglr	f sglr	m plural	f plural
lequel	laquelle	lesquels	lesquelles

If they're used after the prepositions '*à*' or '*de*', they combine with them:

Les chiens avec <u>lesquels</u> il jouait.
The dogs which he was playing with

	m sglr	f sglr	m plural	f plural
de	duquel	de laquelle	desquels	desquelles
à	auquel	à laquelle	auxquels	auxquelles

Ce qui and ce que

Two other relative pronouns, similar to qui and que are:

ce qui — used to replace a phrase which is the *subject* of a sentence

ce que — replaces a phrase which is the *object* of a sentence

> Both mean '*what*' or '*which*'.

  eg: <u>Ce qui</u> est fait est fait   *What's done is done*

     Tu peux penser <u>ce que</u> tu veux   *You can think what you like*

They can be used after tout to mean '*all that*', '*everything that*' or '*anything that*'.

  eg: Tout <u>ce que</u> tu as fait   *Everything that you have done*

Interrogative Pronouns are used to ask questions

These are *important*. Make sure you can *use* and *recognise* all of them in the *Exam*. Qui and que can combine with 'est-ce que', but they still mean the same thing.

Qui?	Who?
Que?	What?
Quoi?	What? ← after a preposition

'<u>À qui?</u>' means '<u>Whose?</u>'

  eg: Ce stylo est <u>à qui</u>?   *Whose is this pen?*

Qui a mangé mon chocolat?

De quoi parlez-vous?

Quel, *quelle*, *quels* and *quelles* all mean *which* or *what*.

  eg: <u>Quel</u> est le chemin le plus court?   *Which is the shortest way?*

Pronouns — boring aren't they...

Phew! That was long, boring and complicated. Unfortunately there's not a lot you can do to make pronouns more interesting, or simple. Just make sure that you know how to use the <u>subject</u> and <u>object</u> pronouns, and can at least <u>recognise</u> the rest. We battle on...

SECTION ONE — ESSENTIAL GRAMMAR

The Present Tense

Yep, now it's _verb time_ — and the key to learning about verbs is to know _how they work_. Verbs are the thing most people _lose valuable marks_ for in the Exam, so take your time and learn them well.

How French Verbs work

There are _three_ types of _regular_ verbs in French:

_-er_ verbs	(ones that end in -er) eg: _regarder_
_-ir_ verbs	_choisir_
_-re_ verbs	_attendre_

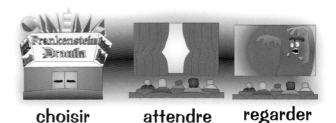

choisir   attendre   regarder

These verb forms are called the _infinitive_. This is the form you'll find when you look up a verb in the _dictionary_. If you then _take off_ the regular ending you'll be left with the '_stem_' of the verb.

INFINITIVE	STEM
regard**er**	regard
chois**ir**	chois
atten**dre**	attend

Each verb in French can have up to _six different forms_ in each tense. These are created by adding different _endings_ to the _stem_ of the verb.

The Present Tense

This is used for any action happening now in the present — and translates as '_I am doing/I do_'.

-er verbs

To form the present tense of _regular_ -er verbs, add the following endings to the verb's stem. eg:

Regarder:

Je regard**e**	-e	Nous regard**ons**	-ons
Tu regard**es**	-es	Vous regard**ez**	-ez
Il regard**e**	-e	Ils regard**ent**	-ent
Elle regard**e**	-e	Elles regard**ent**	-ent
On regard**e**	-e		

NOTE: _il_, _elle_ and _on_ always have the _same_ ending — _on_ means 'it' or 'one'.

Irregular -er Verb Groups — The Magnificent Seven

The big problem with French verbs is that there are loads of _irregular_ ones to learn as well.

1) Verbs which _add_ an _accent_ in the _je_, _tu_, _il_, _elle_, _on_, _ils_, _elles_ forms, eg: _acheter_, _lever_ and _mener_.

Acheter

[stay the same]

j'ach**è**te	nous achetons
tu ach**è**tes	vous achetez
il/elle/on ach**è**te	ils/elles ach**è**tent

2) Verbs where the _accent_ is _reversed_, eg: _espérer_, _considérer_, _répéter_, _préférer_.

Espérer

[stay the same]

j'esp**è**re	nous espérons
tu esp**è**res	vous espérez
il/elle/on esp**è**re	ils/elles esp**è**rent

3) Verbs which _double_ the _last letter_ of the _stem_, eg: _appeler_, _jeter_.

Appeler

[stay the same]

j'appe**ll**e	nous appelons
tu appe**ll**es	vous appelez
il/elle/on appe**ll**e	ils/elles appe**ll**ent

4) Verbs which end _-oyer_ or _-uyer_, y → i eg: _nettoyer_, _ennuyer_, _employer_.

Nettoyer

[stay the same]

Je nett**oi**e	nous nettoyons
tu nett**oi**es	vous nettoyez
il/elle/on nett**oi**e	ils/elles nett**oi**ent

The Present Tense

5) Verbs ending in *-ger*, eg: *manger, nager*. These are regular apart from the <u>nous</u> form, which adds an *'e'* after the *'g'*.

eg: nous mang**e**ons

6) Verbs ending in *-cer*, eg: *commencer, menacer*. These are regular apart from the <u>nous</u> form, where the *'c'* changes to *'ç'*.

eg: nous commen**ç**ons

7) <u>Aller</u> is a very important -er verb, and is *totally irregular*. Typical huh...

je vais	nous allons
tu vas	vous allez
il/elle/on va	ils/elles vont

Nous mangeons notre petit déjeuner

-ir verbs

Regular -ir verbs add the following endings to their stem:

ARRIVÉE

Finir:

je fin**is**	-is	nous fin**issons**	-issons
tu fin**is**	-is	vous fin**issez**	-issez
il/elle/on fin**it**	-it	ils/elles fin**issent**	-issent

There are quite a lot of *irregular* -ir verbs, which means that you've got to learn them all *off by heart*.

Ouvrir	Partir	Venir	Courir
	(also dormir, mentir, sortir, servir)	(also devenir, tenir, retenir)	
j'ouvre	je pars	je viens	je cours
tu ouvres	tu pars	tu viens	tu cours
il/elle/on ouvre	il/elle/on part	il/elle/on vient	il/elle/on court
nous ouvrons	nous partons	nous venons	nous courons
vous ouvrez	vous partez	vous venez	vous courez
ils/elles ouvrent	ils/elles partent	ils/elles viennent	ils/elles courent

Verbs ending in *-oir* are <u>all</u> irregular — just what you wanted to know.

Avoir		Devoir		Pouvoir	
j'ai	nous avons	je dois	nous devons	je peux	nous pouvons
tu as	vous avez	tu dois	vous devez	tu peux	vous pouvez
il/elle/on a	ils/elles ont	il/elle/on doit	ils/elles doivent	il/elle/on peut	ils/elles peuvent

-re verbs

Regular -re verbs add these endings to their stem — note that the il/elle/on form has *no new ending*:

Vendre:

je vend**s**	-s	nous vend**ons**	-ons
tu vend**s**	-s	vous vend**ez**	-ez
il/elle/on vend		ils/elles vend**ent**	-ent

There are a lot of *irregular* -re verbs.

être		dire		faire	
je suis	nous sommes	je dis	nous disons	je fais	nous faisons
tu es	vous êtes	tu dis	vous dites	tu fais	vous faites
il/elle/on est	ils/elles sont	il/elle/on dit	ils/elles disent	il/elle/on fait	ils/elles font

Verbs are a pain in the neck — so don't tense up...

And that's the present tense. You'll use this tense a lot, so make sure that you know it really well, especially the *irregular verbs*, which you've just gotta *learn*.

Reflexive Verbs

Reflexive verbs are used for actions you do *to yourself* — they're formed like any other verb but they've also got to have a *reflexive pronoun*. Make sure you learn how to form these *carefully*.

Reflexive Verbs **have a** Reflexive Pronoun **in front of them**

Remember — these are about doing something *to yourself*, eg: '*se laver*':

Se Laver	to Wash Oneself
je <u>me</u> lave	I wash <u>myself</u>
tu <u>te</u> laves	you wash <u>yourself</u>
il <u>se</u> lave	he washes <u>himself</u>
nous <u>nous</u> lavons	we wash <u>ourselves</u>
vous <u>vous</u> lavez	you wash <u>yourself/selves</u>
ils <u>se</u> lavent	they wash <u>themselves</u>

Reflexive Pronouns	
me	nous
te	vous
se	se

1) Reflexive verbs are easy to form — phew. They're the same as regular verbs except they always have a *reflexive pronoun* in front of them. They take the same endings as regular *-er*, *-ir* and *-re* verbs in all tenses — although a few of them are irregular.

2) Loads of the verbs you need to describe your *daily routine* are reflexives — and you've been using reflexive verbs since your first French lesson — the verb *s'appeler* is reflexive:

Je <u>m'</u>appelle...   I call myself... — my name is...
Comment <u>t'</u>appelles-tu?   What do you call yourself?

TWO *DEAD USEFUL* REFLEXIVE VERBS

se sentir (to feel emotionally)
eg: Je <u>me</u> sens triste   *I feel sad*
          Il <u>se</u> sent mal   *He feels ill*
se lever (to get up)
eg: Je <u>me</u> lève à 8 heures   *I get up at 8 o'clock*

Perfect (Past) Tense of Reflexive Verbs

This sounds really tricky — but it's *not*. You'll need to come back to it when you've looked at P.18. Reflexives *always* form the *perfect tense* using *être*. They form past participles the *same* way as normal verbs. Because they use être, the past participle must *agree* with the *subject* of the verb.

REMEMBER — The *reflexive pronoun* always goes *before* the bit of être, eg:

SE LAVER   (past participle = lavé)

je <u>me</u> suis lavé(e)	nous <u>nous</u> sommes lavé(e)<u>s</u>
tu <u>t'</u>es lavé(e)	vous <u>vous</u> êtes lavé(e)(s)
il <u>s'</u>est lavé	ils <u>se</u> sont lavé<u>s</u>
elle <u>s'</u>est lavée	elles <u>se</u> sont lavé<u>es</u>

Quand était la dernière fois que tu t'es lavé?

Je me suis lavé l'année dernière!

Learn about reflexives — you'll be helping yourself...

Examiners like it if you use reflexive verbs, especially in the past tense. The *pronouns* make them a bit tricky, but if you practise using them a lot you'll get the hang of it in no time. As long as you remember that they always use '*être*' in the past tense you'll have no trouble impressing that examiner. Don't forget, the past participle has to *agree* with the person doing the action.

The Future Tense

The future tense means what it says — what you _plan_ to do in the _future_. There are _two main forms_.

The Future Tense proper is pretty darn easy

This is the main way of forming the future tense — and it translates as '_I will do something_'.

Forming the Future Tense

1) The future tense _endings_ are:

je	-ai	nous	-ons
tu	-as	vous	-ez
il/elle/on	-a	ils/elles	-ont

NOTE: these endings are _identical_ to the present tense of _avoir_ (except for the nous and vous forms).

2) These endings are added to the infinitive of regular verbs.

    a) _-er_ and _-ir_ verbs — simply stick the right ending onto the end of the infinitive.

        eg: Je regarder_ai_   _I will watch_
            Il grandir_a_   _He will grow_

    b) _-re_ verbs — knock off the final _-e_, and add the right ending.

        eg: Nous prendr_ons_   _We will take_
            Tu suivr_as_   _You will follow_

3) Amazingly there are only a few important _irregular verbs_ in the future tense — that makes a change.

4) They use the _same endings_ but have a _different_ '_stem_' (the bit you add the ending onto):

VERB	STEM	VERB	STEM
aller	_ir_	pouvoir	_pourr_
avoir	_aur_	recevoir	_recevr_
devoir	_devr_	savoir	_saur_
dire	_dir_	tenir	_tiendr_
être	_ser_	venir	_viendr_
faire	_fer_	voir	_verr_
falloir	_faudr_	envoyer	_enverr_
mourir	_mourr_	vouloir	_voudr_

eg: J'_irai_ en France l'été prochain.
    I will go to France next summer
    Quand il _aura_ dix-huit ans, il _ira_ à l'université.
    When he is eighteen, he will go to university

REMEMBER: the future tense of any verb always has an '_r_' before the future ending. If you haven't got one, you've gone wrong somewhere!

Using the Future Tense

Some tremendous phrases that might come in handy if you want to talk about the future are:

    dans l'avenir .....   (In the future...)
    d'abord   (First of all)
    ensuite   (then)

Always use the future tense to talk about future plans, eg: what you plan to do when you leave school, or where you're planning to go on holiday next year.

Immediate Future — Aller Faire

This is _even easier_, but you'll get more marks if you _use_ and _recognise_ the future tense proper. The immediate future translates as '_going to do something_':

present tense of aller + infinitive

Nous allons faire le ménage!

Je vais faire une promenade   I'm going to go for a walk
Il va jouer au football samedi   He's going to play football on Saturday
Nous allons faire le ménage   We're going to do the housework

Going over it again — back to the future...

This is probably one of the _easiest_ tenses to learn, so make sure you use it at every opportunity in the exam. It'll impress the examiners if you use a mixture of regular and irregular verbs, and using the _immediate future_ as well makes you sound more French.

The Perfect Tense

This is the basic _past_ tense form. It's dead important you learn it — it's in _all sections_ of the _Exam_.

Perfect Tense _Verbs need an_ Auxiliary Verb

Right, you'll need 2 things to form this tense — the present tense of either _avoir_ or _être_ AND the _past participle_ of the verb (see below). The bit of avoir or être is called the '_auxiliary_' verb.

Perfect tense = **present tense of avoir/être + past participle of verb**

1) _How to form the_ Past Participle _of a verb_

Past participles are just the stem of the verb with a special past tense ending. So learn them now.

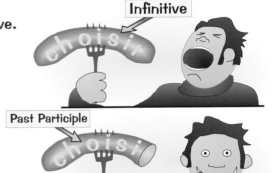

Infinitive

Past Participle

a) **-ER VERBS**

Step 1 — Knock the _-er_ off the end of the infinitive.
Step 2 — Add _-é_ to the end.
eg: regard<u>er</u> → regard<u>é</u>

b) **-IR VERBS**

Step 1 — Knock the _-r_ off the infinitive.
eg: chois<u>ir</u> → chois<u>i</u>

c) **-RE VERBS**

Step 1 — Knock the _-re_ off the infinitive.
Step 2 — Add _-u_ to the end.
eg: vend<u>re</u> → vend<u>u</u>

The Really Annoying Bit — those pesky Irregular _Past Participles_

These verbs form the perfect tense the same way as above, but their _past participles_ are irregular.

Verb	Past Participle	Translation
avoir	eu	had
boire	bu	drank
conduire	conduit	drove
connaître	connu	knew
courir	couru	ran
craindre	craint	feared
devoir	dû	had to
dire	dit	said
écrire	écrit	wrote
être	été	have been

Verb	Past Participle	Translation
faire	fait	did
lire	lu	read
mettre	mis	put
ouvrir	ouvert	opened
pouvoir	pu	have been able
prendre	pris	took
rire	ri	laughed
savoir	su	knew
voir	vu	saw
vouloir	voulu	wanted

2) _There are only_ Two Auxiliary _verbs —_ Avoir or Être

a) _Avoir_ — Just about every sensible regular French verb uses avoir to form the perfect tense.

REGARDER — to look at	
j'ai regardé	_I looked at_
tu as regardé	_you looked at_
il/elle/on a regardé	_he/she/one looked at_
nous avons regardé	_we looked at_
vous avez regardé	_you looked at_
ils/elles ont regardé	_they looked at_

CHOISIR — to choose
j'ai choisi
tu as choisi
il/elle/on a choisi
nous avons choisi
vous avez choisi
ils/elles ont choisi

VENDRE — to sell
j'ai vend<u>u</u>
tu as vend<u>u</u>
il/elle/on a vend<u>u</u>
nous avons vend<u>u</u>
vous avez vend<u>u</u>
ils/elles ont vend<u>u</u>

The Perfect Tense

b) Fifteen Awkward Verbs use *Être* to form the *perfect tense*.

Unfortunately they're fifteen *dead common verbs*, so you'll need to *learn* them really well:

Verb		Past Participle	Examples:
Aller	(to go)	allé	**Aller — to go**
Arriver	(to arrive)	arrivé	
Descendre	(to go down)	descendu	
Devenir	(to become)	devenu	
Entrer	(to go in)	entré	
Monter	(to go up)	monté	
Mourir	(to die)	mort	
Naître	(to be born)	né	
Partir	(to leave)	parti	
Rentrer	(to go back)	rentré	
Retourner	(to return)	retourné	
Rester	(to stay)	resté	
Sortir	(to go out)	sorti	
Tomber	(to fall)	tombé	
Venir	(to come)	venu	

Examples:

Aller — to go

je	suis	allé(e)
tu	es	allé(e)
il	est	allé
elle	est	allée
nous	sommes	allé(e)s
vous	êtes	allé(e)(s)
ils	sont	allés
elles	sont	allées

Sortir — to go out

je	suis	sorti(e)
tu	es	sorti(e)
il	est	sorti
elle	est	sortie
nous	sommes	sorti(e)s
vous	êtes	sorti(e)(s)
ils	sont	sortis
elles	sont	sorties

REMEMBER: Reflexive verbs always use être to form the perfect tense

With *Être* as the Auxiliary Verb, the Past Participle must Agree:

When you use *être* to form the perfect tense, the past participle has to *agree* with the subject of the verb, just like an adjective.

Add *e* if the subject is *feminine singular*
Add *s* if the subject is *masculine plural*
Add *es* if the subject is *feminine plural*

Je suis né à Londres.

eg: *Je* suis *né* à Londres.
     I was born in London
     L'été dernier *elle* est allé*e* en France.
     Last summer she went to France
     Nous sommes arrivé*s* à quatre heures.
     We arrived at four o'clock

Be careful with '*VOUS*', as it can refer to *one person*, or *more than one person*

eg: Vous (le professeur) êtes resté à la maison hier soir?
     Did you stay at home last night?
     Vous (les étudiants) êtes allé*s* au cinéma.
     You went to the cinema

The Perfect Tense — it's truly flawless...

People do often lose marks on the this in the Exams, which is silly considering that it's actually pretty *easy*. You need to know the present tense of *avoir* and *être* and *which one* of these a verb takes to form the perfect tense. You are going to *have* to use the perfect tense in the Exams — so the bottom line is you've got to learn EVERYTHING on this page. Learn and enjoy.

The Imperfect Tense

This is *another past tense*. It's used for actions in the past that *were ongoing* — eg: I was *eating*.

Three Easy Steps *to forming the* Imperfect Tense

1) Take the present tense *'nous'* form of the verb.
2) Knock off the *-ons*.
3) Add the correct *imperfect ending*.
4) The imperfect endings are:

Knock the 'ons' from the nous form of the present tense →

ALLONS

je	-ais	nous	-ions
tu	-ais	vous	-iez
il/elle/on	-ait	ils/elles	-aient

A few Examples:

nous faisons → je fais**ais**   *I was doing*
nous parlons → tu parl**ais**   *you were speaking*
nous buvons → ils buv**aient**   *we were drinking*

eg: *ALLER* — (to go)
j'all**ais**   *I was going*
tu all**ais**   *you were going*
il/elle/on all**ait**   *he/she/one was going*
nous all**ions**   *we were going*
vous all**iez**   *you were going*
ils/elles all**aient**   *they were going*

SOME UNBELIEVABLY GOOD NEWS — there's only *one irregular verb* in the imperfect tense.

It's *ÊTRE*:

j'ét**ais**	nous ét**ions**
tu ét**ais**	vous ét**iez**
il/elle/on ét**ait**	ils/elles ét**aient**

Être uses the *same* imperfect *endings*, but has a *different* imperfect *stem*.

When to Use **the Imperfect Tense** — *was, did, used to do*

The imperfect tense can be translated as '*I was doing something*', '*I did something*' or '*I used to do something*'. You really need to know it for the Exams so you can:

1) Describe something you *used to do* by habit/repeatedly in the past.
   eg: J'*allais* au cinéma tous les jeudis.   *I used to go to the cinema every Thursday*

2) Descriptions in *the past*, including descriptions of your *state* (eg: emotions, physical states).

eg: J'*étais* triste   *I was sad*   —   state, an emotion
Il *faisait* chaud   *It was hot*   —   description
Il *pleuvait*   *It was raining*   —   description

3) Describe an *action* which was *still going on* at the moment you're talking about in the past. This is like English '*I was ....ing*'.
   eg: Pendant que je *regardais* la télévision, mon frère *écoutait* la radio.
   While I was watching television, my brother was listening to the radio

The *Difference* between the *Perfect* and the *Imperfect*

1) The *IMPERFECT* tense is used for *descriptions*, *past habits* and *continuous actions in the past*.
2) The *PERFECT* tense is used to talk about actions that have been *completed*.
So the imperfect tense *'sets the scene'* while the perfect tense describes the *key events*. Here's a smashing example: **Pendant que** je lisais **mon livre**, quelqu'un a frappé **à la porte**.
     While I was reading my book, someone knocked at the door

Verbs — the only time you'll want something imperfect...

Don't be alarmed, this is really pretty easy. You'll already know the present tense, so all you have to do now is *learn* a set of *endings*, and the imperfect stem for the verb *être*.

The Conditional Tense

Phew — yet another tense, but this one's great for getting you extra marks in the Oral Exam. The _conditional tense_ is used in '_if_' or '_whether_' sentences and _reported speech_ for things you _would do_.

Forming the Conditional Tense — would, could or should

The rule for _forming_ the conditional tense is:

future stem + imperfect tense ending

So spend some time learning the _future stems_ of regular verbs:

A reminder of the _imperfect endings_:

je	-ais	nous	-ions
tu	-ais	vous	-iez
il	-ait	ils	-aient
elle	-ait	elles	-aient

With _-er_ verbs you use the _infinitive_ form: <u>inviter</u>   _invite_
With _-ir_ verbs you use the _infinitive_ form: <u>choisir</u>   _choose_
With _-re_ verbs you _remove_ the final _e_: <u>vendr</u>   _sell_

Some verbs have irregular future stems, but the endings never change

aller	(to go)	→	j'<u>ir</u>ais	(I would go)
avoir	(to have)	→	tu <u>aur</u>ais	(you would have)
être	(to be)	→	il <u>ser</u>ait	(he would be)
faire	(to do)	→	elle <u>fer</u>ait	(she would do)
pouvoir	(to be able)	→	nous <u>pourr</u>ions	(we <u>could</u> / we would be able to)
venir	(to come)	→	on <u>viendr</u>ait	(one/we would come)
voir	(to see)	→	nous <u>verr</u>ions	(we would see)
vouloir	(to want)	→	vous <u>voudr</u>iez	(you would like)
devoir	(to have to)	→	ils <u>devr</u>aient	(they <u>should</u> / they would have to)
s'asseoir	(to sit down)	→	elles s'<u>assiér</u>aient	(they would sit down)

When to Use the Conditional Tense

1) It's used in sentences which begin with '<u>si</u>' (<u>if</u>) when one action _depends_ on certain conditions or circumstances. Study these examples:

Si j'avais assez d'argent, j'<u>irais</u> aux États Unis.   _If I had enough money, I would go to the USA_
S'il pleuvait, nous <u>visiterions</u> un musée.   _If it rained we would visit a museum_

2) It's also used after '<u>si</u>' (when si means '<u>whether</u>') in indirect questions, for example:
Je me demandais s'il <u>gagnerait</u> le prix.   _I wondered whether he would win the prize_
Je ne savais pas si tu <u>trouverais</u> le stylo.   _I didn't know whether you would find the pen_

3) It's used loads in _reported speech_, just like in English, for example:
J'ai dit que je <u>retournerais</u> vers six heures.   _I said that I would return about six o'clock_
Il a déclaré qu'il <u>lutterait</u> contre la pauvreté.   _He declared that he would struggle against poverty_

4) It's used in _time phrases_ where we would use the _imperfect_ tense in English, for example:
Je lui ai dit de monter quand elle <u>serait</u> prête.   _I told her to come up when she was ready_

5) And finally, for _polite requests_ we use the conditional of _vouloir_ everywhere, for example:
Je <u>voudrais</u> une grande glace s'il vous plaît.   _I would like a large ice-cream please_

More tenses than a bodybuilder — that's French ...

Another exciting new tense. It's formed as a hybrid of two tenses that you'll already know, so it won't be too difficult. The table looks tricky, so learn it _bit by bit_ — the _examples_ will help.

The Imperative and the Present Participle

Here are a few key bits of grammar you haven't covered yet — they're dead useful so *learn 'em*.

The Three Uses of the Imperative

1) It's used for giving instructions to *one person you know* — the present tense *tu* form (see P.14).
2) It's also used for instructing *several people/one or more adults* — the present tense *vous* form.
3) You'll definitely need it for making a *suggestion* to do something — the present *nous* form.

It's formed from the present tense minus its subject pronouns (tu, vous and nous) — and there's no final s with the tu form of -er verbs

3) So here's a practice list of examples of *regular* verb imperatives:

	tu form	nous form	vous form
er verb	donne (give)	donnons (let's give)	donnez (give)
ir verb	finis (finish)	finissons (let's finish)	finissez (finish)
re verb	vends (sell)	vendons (let's sell)	vendez (sell)

4) But don't forget the *irregulars*:

	tu form	nous form	vous form
être -to be	sois (be)	soyons (let's be)	soyez (be)
avoir - to have	aie (have)	ayons (let's have)	ayez (have)
savoir - to know	sache (know)	sachons (let's know)	sachez (know)
aller - to go	va (go)	allons (let's go)	allez (go)
s'en aller - to go away	va-t'en (go away)	allons-nous-en (let's go away)	allez-vous-en (go away)

6) **SPELLCHECK** Verbs whose stem ends in '*g*' add on '*e*' before the *nous* ending (-ons)
Verbs whose stem ends in '*c*' change to '*ç*' before *-ons*.

mangeons *let's eat*   commençons *let's start*

7) Sometimes you need the imperative to tell a person to do something for you, eg: give you the paper. For that you must use an *emphatic pronoun* (see P.12).

Donne-moi le journal!

REMEMBER: With the imperative the emphatic pronoun goes *after* the verb and NOT before — except for *negative imperatives* which have an ordinary *object pronoun* and normal word order (pronoun *before* the verb).

Ordinary sentence = tu *me* donnes le journal   *you give me the 'paper*
Imperative = donne-*moi* le journal!   *give me the newspaper*
Negative Imperative = ne *me* donne pas le journal!   *don't give me the 'paper*

Present Participle — the process of doing something

Right, this is the way you translate all those ace English words that end with *-ing*. Here's how to form them:

Present tense nous form of verb minus -ons + ant

eg: jou(ons) + ant → jou*ant*   *playing*
     dis(ons) + ant → dis*ant*   *saying*
     rougiss(ons) + ant → rougiss*ant* *blushing*

BUT remember the *irregulars*:

avoir	→	ayant	(having)
être	→	étant	(being)
savoir	→	sachant	(knowing)

1) The *present participle + en* means 'while/by/on doing something' — it's the only preposition used with the form: eg: Il lisait *en déjeunant* *He read while having his lunch*

2) The present participle can also be used as an *adjective*. When it is, it must *agree* with the noun like *any other* adjective, eg: *une* dame charman*te*   *a charming lady*
                                                                  des châteaux intéressan*ts*   *interesting castles*

The Pluperfect Tense

The pluperfect tense is sometimes called the *past perfect tense*. It means what someone *had* done.

Forming *the amazing Pluperfect Tense*

You'll only need: **Imperfect tense of avoir/être + past participle**

1) AVOIR

j'avais	nous avions
tu avais	vous aviez
il avait	ils avaient
elle avait	elles avaient

2) ÊTRE

j'étais	nous étions
tu étais	vous étiez
il était	ils étaient
elle était	elles étaient

REMEMBER the *Recipes* for *regular PAST PARTICIPLES*:

1) For <u>er</u> verbs: take the infinitive, chop off the -er and add a little -é.
2) For <u>ir</u> verbs: take the infinitive and cut off the -r.
3) For <u>re</u> verbs: take infinitive, squeeze off the -re and add a wee drop of -u.
4) For <u>oir</u> verbs: take the infinitive, cut out the -oir and sprinkle a little -u on the end.

Some Tricky Examples of the PLUPERFECT:

Elles s'étaient levées de bonne heure	*They had got up early*
J'avais acheté un pull	*I had bought a sweater*
Il avait marché toute la journée	*He had walked all day*
Nous avions voulu aller en France	*We had wanted to go to France*

Another Use *of the Pluperfect — 'si' clauses*

You need the pluperfect with the <u>CONDITIONAL</u> in 'if' sentences (see P.21)

Examples: S'il *avait apporté* sa raquette, nous aurions joué au tennis.
If he had brought his raquet, we would have played tennis
S'ils *étaient montés* à la colline, ils auraient vu le château.
If they had climbed the hill, they would have seen the castle

The Imperfect *means 'had been' after* depuis *and* il y a

1) After the *time phrases*: *depuis* and *il y a* (for + amount of time), the *IMPERFECT* tense is used instead of pluperfect.

   eg: *Depuis* combien de temps attendais-tu?   *How long had you been waiting?*
        Il y a une demi-heure que j'attendais.   *I had been waiting for half an hour*

2) You can avoid the pluperfect tense by using a *preposition* followed by a *past infinitive*. Here are some examples to illustrate this:

<u>Après avoir mangé</u> nous sommes allés au cinéma.   *After we had eaten we went to the cinema*
<u>Après être sorti</u>, j'ai rencontré mes amis.   *After I had gone out, I met my friends*

3) *The past participle* of the pluperfect must *agree* with any *direct object pronouns* (P.10).

   The rule is:

with *feminine singular* + *e* ...	
with *masculine plural* + *s* ...	...on to past participle
with *feminine plural* + *es* ...	

   eg: *Les souvenirs, qu'il avait achetés, étaient chers.*   *The souvenirs which he had bought were expensive*

A room of B-list celebs — full of has beens...

Don't look at the whole page and think "I'll never learn all that" — look at it <u>one</u> section at a *time*. The imperative's actually pretty easy, and the pluperfect's like two tenses at once.

Savoir, Connaître and Pouvoir

Here are three smashing verbs that people often get confused — so learn them right now.

Savoir — to know, know how

1) _Savoir_ means '_to know_' with a noun, an object pronoun or introducing a phrase, in the sense of: being aware of/having learnt/having been informed about

Make really sure you understand these examples:

Elle _sait_ la réponse à la question	She knows the answer to the question
Savez-vous son adresse?	Do you know his address?
Tu _savais_ la leçon	You knew the lesson
Je _sais_ comment le faire	I know how to do it
Nous ne l'avons _su_ qu'hier	We only knew it yesterday
Je ne _savais_ pas s'il irait	I did not know if he would go
Savez-vous l'heure du train?	Do you know the time of the train?

Je sais le latin

2) _Savoir_ followed by an _infinitive_ means 'to know how to do something', in the sense of a skill, eg:

Il _sait_ faire du ski
He knows how to ski

Elle ne _sait_ pas lire
She cannot read

Je _sais_ conduire
I can drive

3) The _conditional_ of savoir, in the _negative_, but _without pas_, can be used to replace the negative present tense of pouvoir, eg: Je ne _saurais_ vous l'expliquer _I cannot explain it to you_

Connaître — to know, be familiar with

Connaître means _to know_ a person or place — to 'be familiar with' or 'have an understanding of', eg:

Je _connais_ Paris	I know Paris
Il ne _connaît_ pas cette ville	He doesn't know this town
Nous _connaissons_ le droit	We know law
Tu _connais_ mon ami?	Do you know my friend?
Ils _connaissent_ le bonheur	They know happiness

Je connais la lune.

Pouvoir — to be able to (the three P's)

Pouvoir (_to be able to/can_) has three very important meanings and they all begin with P:

1) The _Physical Ability_ to do something.

eg: Il ne _pouvait_ pas le supporter.
Je _peux_ marcher à l'aide d'une canne.
Elle ne _peut_ pas venir ce matin.

He could not stand it
I can walk with the help of a stick
She cannot come this morning

2) _Permission_ to do something.

eg: On _peut_ prendre des photos ici.
Tu ne _pourrais_ pas rester demain.
J'ai _pu_ laisser mon sac chez elle.

You can take photos here
You could not stay tomorrow
I've been able to leave my bag at her house

3) _Possibility_ of something being the case.

eg: Cela _peut_ arriver.
La fille _pouvait_ avoir seize ans.
Il _pourra_ peut-être vous prêter l'auto.

That can happen
The girl could have been sixteen
He may be able to lend you the car

Pouvoir — make sure you get your three P's sweet...

Three lovely verbs that you need to sort out. Don't forget the difference between _savoir_ and _connaître_, and make sure that you know the three meanings of _pouvoir_...

Negative Expressions

Right — the _negative_ in French is pretty complicated because you need _two bits_ — a _ne_ and another bit. So start by learning the common examples below:

ne ..... pas	_not_	ne ..... personne	_nobody, not anybody_
ne ..... point	_not, not at all_	personne ..... ne	_nobody, not anybody_
ne ..... plus	_no more, no longer_	ne ..... rien	_nothing, not anything_
ne .... que	_only, nothing but_	rien ..... ne	_nothing, not anything_
ne ..... guère	_hardly, scarcely_	ne ..... aucun(e)	_not any, not one_
ne ..... jamais	_never, not ever_	aucun(e) ..... ne	_not any, not one_
ne ... ni ... ni	_neither ... nor_	ne ..... nul(le)	_not any, not one_
ni ... ni ... ne	_neither ... nor_	ne ..... nulle part	_nowhere, not anywhere_

1) The _RULE_ for making negative sentences is:

subject + ne + verb + pas/point etc

The _ne_ and _pas_ (or point, que etc.) always go _either side_ of the verb.

Study these examples:

Je _ne_ regarde _pas_ la télé ce soir	_I am not watching TV tonight_
Il _ne_ va _jamais_ à l'étranger	_He never goes abroad_
Le bus _ne_ part _qu'_à midi	_The bus doesn't leave until midday_
Tu _ne_ le vois _nulle part_	_You don't see it anywhere_
Il _n'_y en a _plus_	_There are no more_

2) If you start with _NO ONE_ or _NOTHING_, the rule is: **personne/rien + _ne_ + _verb_**

For example:
Personne _n'_arrive en retard — _No-one arrives late_
Aucun élève _ne_ reçoit la lettre — _No pupil gets the letter_

3) With compound verbs, like the _PERFECT_ and _PLUPERFECT_ tenses, the _ne_ part of the negative goes _in front_ of the auxiliary verbs avoir and être (see P.8 and P.23).

For example:
Personne _n'_est sorti — _No-one went out_
Je _n'_ai _rien_ acheté — _I bought nothing_

4) _DOUBLE_ negatives have just _one_ ne before the verb:

For example:
Elle _ne_ dit _jamais rien_ en français — _She never says anything in French_
Je _ne_ voyais _plus personne_ — _I could no longer see anyone_

5) For negatives with _INFINITIVES_: **ne + pas + infinitive**

eg:. Il m'a dit de _ne pas_ attendre — _He told me not to wait_

6) There are some everyday spoken expressions which use pas, but have _NO VERB_.

pas un mot!	_not a word!_
pas encore!	_not yet!_
pas moi!	_not me!_
pas de problème	_no problem_

7) Some common expressions use ne, although the sense of the sentence is _NOT NEGATIVE_.

For example:
Il y a longtemps que je _ne_ l'ai vu — _It's a long time since I saw him_
Elle est plus âgée que tu _ne_ penses — _She is older than you think_

What a page — more negatives than a camera shop...

First of all, you need to know where the two bits of the negative go. You also need to learn the negative words in the orange box and the _examples_ and _exceptions_. Take it step by step.

Numbers, Age and Telling The Time

When Your Number's Up

0	zéro	20	vingt	80	quatre-vingts
1	un, une	21	vingt et un	81	quatre-vingt-un
2	deux	22	vingt-deux	82	quatre-vingt-deux
3	trois	23	vingt-trois	90	quatre-vingt-dix
4	quatre	24	vingt-quatre	91	quatre-vingt-onze
5	cinq	25	vingt-cinq	92	quatre-vingt-douze
6	six	26	vingt-six	100	cent
7	sept	27	vingt-sept	101	cent un
8	huit	28	vingt-huit	105	cent cinq
9	neuf	29	vingt-neuf	115	cent quinze
10	dix	30	trente	160	cent soixante
11	onze	31	trente et un	200	deux cents
12	douze	40	quarante	211	deux cent onze
13	treize	41	quarante et un	400	quatre cents
14	quatorze	50	cinquante	725	sept cent vingt-cinq
15	quinze	60	soixante	1000	mille
16	seize	70	soixante-dix	1302	mille trois cent deux
17	dix-sept	71	soixante et onze	5000	cinq mille
18	dix-huit	72	soixante-douze	1,000,000	un million
19	dix-neuf	79	soixante-dix-neuf	1,000,000,000	un milliard

The RULE for ordinal numbers is:— **number + ième** eg: *deuxième* *(second)*

The EXCEPTION to the rule is:— *premier/première* *(first)*

How to give your Age (or pretend to...)

J'ai un an

You'll definitely be asked "*Quel âge as-tu?*" *(How old are you?)*

To say how old you are use: **avoir + number + ans**

J'*ai seize* ans *I am 16*

Ma soeur *a onze* ans *My sister is 11*

Telling the Time — les minutes et les heures

Work from the whole hour, add on the times to and past the hour. The RULES are:

1) The *full* hour — **il est + number + heure(s)** eg: *il est trois heures* *it is three o'clock*

EXCEPTIONS to this are: il est midi *it is midday* and il est minuit *it is midnight*

2) *Half past* the hour — **number + heure/s + et demie** eg: *deux heures et demie* *half past two*

EXCEPTIONS: 'midi et demi' *(half past twelve midday)*, 'minuit et demi' *(half past twelve midnight)*

3) For times *past* the hour — **number of hours + heure/s + number of minutes past** **or** **+ et quart**

eg: trois heures dix *ten past three*   cinq heures et quart *quarter past five*

4) For times *to* the hour — **number + heure/s + moins + number of minutes to** **or** **+ le quart**

eg: huit heures moins vingt *twenty to eight*   une heure moins le quart *quarter to one*

Jokes about clocks — it's all comic timing...

Numbers are really, really *important*. They will come up *everywhere*. Time, age, train timetables, your school year, phone numbers. So, you've just gotta learn them. Do it *now*.

Days, Months, Weather and Seasons

Les Jours de la Semaine — Days of the Week

The days of the week are always written with a _small letter_ in French.

Monday	Tuesday	Wednesday	Thursday	Friday	Saturday	Sunday
lundi	mardi	mercredi	jeudi	vendredi	samedi	dimanche

Other useful expressions to learn are:

aujourd'hui	_today_
quotidien(ne)	_daily_
hier	_yesterday_
demain	_tomorrow_

Tu vas te faire couper les cheveux aujourd'hui?

Je l'ai fait hier!

Les Mois de l'Année — Months of the Year

The months are also written with a _small letter_ in French.

janvier	_January_	juillet	_July_
février	_February_	août	_August_
mars	_March_	septembre	_September_
avril	_April_	octobre	_October_
mai	_May_	novembre	_November_
juin	_June_	décembre	_December_

Dates

With the exception of the _first_, when you use '_premier_', the rule for making the date is:

le + number + month

eg: le premier février   _1st February_
      le neuf mai   _9th May_
      le vingt et un août   _21st August_

Le Temps — the Weather

To ask what the weather's like: eg:

Quel temps fait-il?

il fait beau	_it's nice weather_
il fait soleil	_it's sunny_
il fait chaud	_it's hot_

il fait mauvais	_it's bad weather_
il fait du brouillard	_it's foggy_
il fait froid	_it's cold_
il pleut	_it's raining_
il gèle	_it's freezing/icy_
il est nuageux	_it's cloudy_
il neige	_it's snowing_
il y a de l'orage	_it's stormy_
il fait du vent	_it's windy_

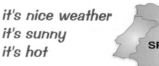

Les Saisons — the Seasons

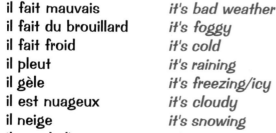

Le printemps - Spring

L'automne - Autumn

L'été - Summer

L'hiver - Winter

To say '_in_' with a season:

use 'au' with printemps:-
au printemps   (in the Spring)

use 'en' minus the article for the rest:-
en été   (in the Summer)

Learn about weather — get yourself on the map...

All this vocabulary is really _important_ — weather _will_, without a shadow of a doubt, appear in the Exams — make sure you learn _all of it_. If you can, read 'un météo' (a weather forecast) in a French newspaper to see weather words work.

Feelings and Opinions

OK — it's time for you to express yourself. This is where you can pick up loads of Exam marks.

Des Sentiments — Feelings

1) The simplest way to express _feelings/emotions_ is: **être + adjective**

2) To express _mood_:

de bonne humeur   _in a good mood_
de mauvaise humeur   _in a bad mood_

3) There are also several _reflexive_ verbs which can be used to express feelings and emotions.

eg: _se_ fâcher   _to get angry_
     je _me_ fâche   _I get angry_
     _s_'énerver   _to get annoyed_
     il _m_'énerve   _he annoys me_
     _s_'agacer   _to make/get mad_
     ça _m_'agace   _that makes me mad_

4) A _general_ verb to express your feelings is:

se sentir + emotion/state of health

CAREFUL — reflexive verb!

Je me sens malade
(I feel ill)   Tu te sens en forme
(You feel fit)

Expressing Opinions — saying what you think

1) To express your personal opinions you can use several verbs + que.

penser	_to think_
croire	_to believe_
trouver	_to find_

2) For alternative ways of stating your opinion the following phrases are useful:

à + possessive adjective + avis (m)   (in .... opinion)

<u>à</u> mon <u>avis</u>   _in my opinion_   <u>à</u> son <u>avis</u>   _in his opinion_
<u>à</u> l'<u>avis</u> de mes parents   _in my parents' opinion_

<u>selon</u> moi   _according to me_
<u>selon</u> lui   _according to him_

<u>quant à</u> moi   _as far as I'm concerned_
<u>quant à</u> mes copains/copines   _as far as my friends are concerned_

My opinion on intolerance — I really can't stand it...

Now you can express yourself fully and say what you really feel. Learn the three ways to say _how you feel_ and the two ways to _express an opinion_. Go on... lay your emotions bare.

Revision Summary for Section One

Phew, the mother of all sections is over — and now it's time for some fantastically awesome revision questions. I know it's boring but it's the only way to see what you know. If you can do these forty questions then you'll be sorted for the Exams. Grammar is the hardest bit of French and you've got to get it learned now. Remember — you must go back over any topics you're not clear on. If you want to do well you've got to get them learned perfectly — so get going.

1) What's the key difference between nouns in French and in English?
2) What are the plural forms of: a) orange b) jeu c) journal d) nez e) oeil?
3) Give the three words (indefinite articles) that mean 'a' or 'an'. When are they used?
4) How would you say: a) a little wine b) more chocolate c) too many vegetables.
5) What is an adjective? How do adjectives agree with nouns? Give two examples.
6) Give the masculine and feminine plural forms of: a) heureux b) vieux c) bon d) tout.
7) Name five adjectives that come before the noun in sentences.
8) What do cher, grand and pauvre mean: a) before the noun b) after the noun?
9) What are the three ways to say 'my'? What's the difference? When would you use them?
10) How would you say: a) this bird b) these apples c) this house?
11) What does an adverb do? How do you form regular adverbs in French? Give the forms of four of the exceptions to this rule.
12) What's the difference between: a) bon and bien b) mauvais and mal?
13) Give the five basic question words in French.
14) What are the three ways of comparing things in French? Give an example.
15) How do you form the superlative in French? When do you use de?
16) What's the difference between adjectives and adverbs?
17) What do prepositions do? Give three words used to translate 'in' and sentences using them.
18) What does depuis mean: a) with the present tense b) with the imperfect tense?
19) What are conjunctions? Give five examples and five sentences using them.
20) What is a pronoun? Where does it go in the sentence?
21) Make a table of subject pronouns, direct object pronouns and indirect object pronouns. Give four verbs that take the indirect object in French (remember the preposition they take).
22) What are emphatic pronouns? Give three examples.
23) What's the difference between qui and que? What does dont mean?
24) What kind of pronouns are used to ask questions? How are they formed?
25) What are the three regular types of present tense verbs? Give two examples of each.
26) How are reflexive verbs formed? Give three examples in full.
27) How are reflexive verbs formed in the past tense? Give an example.
28) Give examples of three regular past participles. Then give examples of eight irregular forms.
29) Give four examples of: a) perfect tense using avoir b) perfect tense using être.
30) What's the difference between the perfect and the imperfect tense? How is the imperfect formed? Which is the only irregular form?
31) Give two methods for forming the future tense, and three examples of each.
32) When is the conditional tense used? How is it formed?
33) When is the imperative used? Give three forms of: a) a regular imperative b) an irregular.
34) What is the pluperfect? Give two examples. When can the imperfect be used instead?
35) Give three meanings of: a) savoir b) pouvoir. What does connaître mean?
36) Give five examples of sentences with common negative phrases.
37) Describe what winter is like using at least six different weather phrases.
38) List the days, months and seasons of the year.
39) What are the three key factors to remember about adjectives?
40) Using two different forms, say how studying French makes you feel.

Self and Family

You've really got a chance to get _easy marks_ in the Exam with this topic — the trick is to _work out_ what you're going to say about yourself and your family and _practise_ it. It's the only way.

Questions about Yourself

You'll be replying to questions from the examiner — practise answering quickly and clearly, eg:

Comment t'appelles-tu? Quel âge as-tu? Parle-moi de toi. Où est-ce que tu habites?

(What is your name?) _(How old are you?)_ _(Tell me about yourself.)_ _(Where do you live?)_

Rehearse all this so that you don't get lost for words on the day

eg: Je m'appelle John. _My name is John_
J'ai seize ans. _I am sixteen_

J'habite dans une ville qui se trouve dans le sud-est de l'Angleterre à Kingston
I live in a town in the south east of England, in Kingston

J'habite à Cardiff, la capitale du Pays de Galles
I live in Cardiff, the capital of Wales

J'habite en Irlande du Nord, dans une ville qui s'appelle Enniskillen
I live in Northern Ireland, in a town called Enniskillen

Parle-moi de ta famille — Information on Your Family

Don't forget your possessive adjectives (see P.3)

Nous sommes quatre personnes dans ma famille
_or_ Il y a quatre personnes dans ma famille
There are four people in my family

mon père, _ma_ mère, _mon_ frère Marc,
_ma_ soeur Anne et _moi_.
If you have more than one brother or sister it's:
mes deux frères, Patrick et Marc or
mes deux soeurs Susan et Emily.

If you are an <u>only child</u> say: _Je suis fils/fille unique_ depending on whether you're a boy or a girl.
To say you are the <u>eldest</u> it's: _Je suis l'aîné(e)_ and if you are the <u>youngest</u> _Je suis le/la benjamin(e)_

If your parents are divorced and you live with your mother or father, you should say:
Mes parents sont divorcés et j'habite avec ma mère/mon père.

What your Parents do for a living

REMEMBER: you say _Mon père est médecin_ or _Ma mère est secrétaire_ without the _un_ or _une_ in front of the profession. Don't get it wrong or you'll lose really important marks.

eg: Mon père est dentiste / facteur / employé de banque / fonctionnaire
My father is a dentist / a postman / a bank employee / a civil servant

Ma mère est médecin / vendeuse / employée de bureau / femme d'affaires
My mother is a doctor / a saleswoman / an office employee / a business woman

For more job titles see P.71

If either your mother or your father works in the legal profession use the following:
Mon père/Ma mère est juge/avocat(e)/avoué(e) = My father/My mother is a judge/barrister/solicitor

Family talk — it's all relative to me...

Talking about yourself should come easily but do _practise_ it — you don't want to be stuck for words in the Exam. Remember how to say you're an only child, or the eldest or whatever.

Family, Friends and Pets

Make sure you have loads of stuff to say about _yourself_ and your _life_ — it'll come in dead handy in the _Oral_ and if you have to write a _letter_. Remember — learn it _now_ and you won't stress out.

1) Tes parents — Talk about your parents

Je _m'entends bien_ avec mes parents
I get on well with my parents

Ma mère est très _gentille_ et on _s'entend bien_
My mother is very nice and we get on well

Je _m'entends_ mieux avec ma mère qu'avec mon père
I get on better with my mother than my father

Mon père est plus _sympa_
My father is nicer

Je _ne m'entends pas_ bien avec mon père/ma mère
I do not get on with my mother/my father

Je le/la trouve _trop sévère_
I find him/her too strict

Mon père est très _strict_. Il _ne me laisse pas_ sortir en semaine
My father is very strict. He doesn't let me go out during the week

Mon père _n'est jamais là_, il travaille tout le temps
My father is never there, he is always working

2) Tes frères et tes soeurs — Brothers and sisters (be polite...)

Yep, brothers and sisters are pretty irritating really — but talking about them gets you _good marks_:

J'aime beaucoup ma petite soeur, mais je la trouve embêtante
I love my younger sister but I find her annoying

If you share a room with your brother or sister:

Je partage une chambre avec ma soeur. J'aime beaucoup ça / je déteste ça parce qu'elle ne range jamais la chambre.
I share a room with my sister. I like this / I hate this because she never tidies the room.

3) Tes ami(e)s — Talking about Friends (not the TV show)

J'ai un/une _meilleur(e) ami(e)_. Il/elle s'appelle...
I have a best friend. He/she is called...

Nous faisons de la musique/jouons _dans l'orchestre de l'école_
We play music/we play in the school orchestra

Mais aussi j'ai beaucoup _d'autres amis_
But I also have a lots of other friends

Nous faisons beaucoup de choses _ensemble_
We do a lot of things together

Nous faisons _du sport_/_du tennis_
We do sport/tennis

Les amis sont _essentiels_ pour moi
Friends are essential in my life

4) Tes animaux domestiques — Pets win (Exam) Prizes

Everyone loves animals — unless they're allergic. These are just _examples_, so work out _your own_:

À la maison, nous avons un _chien_ / un _chat_ / un _lapin_ / un _hamster_ / une _tortue_ / un _oiseau_.
At home we have a dog / a cat / a rabbit / a hamster / a tortoise / a bird

Mon chat est très _intelligent_. Il est _blanc et noir_.
My cat is very clever. He's black and white

J'adore mon chien, il est _tout noir_ et très _mignon_.
I adore my dog. He is all black and very sweet

Je _lui donne à manger_ et _le promène_ tous les jours.   _I feed him and walk him every day_

The key to your Oral Exam — it's all talk...

Remember — don't just learn the stuff on the page. You've got to use the examples to come up with your _own_ answers. Start scribbling some ideas on the page then practise _saying_ them.

Describing Yourself

This is a really good way to get marks — by describing what you _look like_ and what _your character_ is like. You can use this vocab to talk about _other people_ as well.

1) **What's your Shape and Size...**

Use the verb ÊTRE (to be)

Je suis de taille moyenne	_I am of medium height_
Je suis assez / très petit(e)	_I am rather / very small_
Je suis grand(e) et mince	_I am tall and thin_
Je suis assez grand(e) et très mince	_I am rather tall and very thin_
Je me trouve trop petit(e) / gros(se)	_I think I am too small / big_

Je suis grand et mince

Je suis très petite

Je me trouve trop grosse

2) **Facing up to Your Features**

Use the verb AVOIR (to have)

J'ai les yeux bleus/marron/verts/noirs/noisette	_I have blue/brown/green/black/hazel eyes_
J'ai les cheveux blonds/châtains/noirs/roux	_I have blond/brown/black/red hair_
Ils sont raides/bouclés/frisés	_It (my hair) is straight/curly/very curly_

J'ai les yeux bleus et les cheveux blonds

Je suis couvert de tâches de rousseur

Je suis très bronzée

Je suis couvert(e) de tâches de rousseur	_I am covered with freckles_
J'ai deux grandes fossettes	_I have two dimples_
Je suis très bronzé(e)	_I am very tanned_
J'ai la peau brune	_I have dark skin_

3) **I'm the Greatest — what're you like...**

Talking about _other people's characters_ can be a lot of fun — but you should start by looking at _your own_. I know it's a pain to have to talk about your _good_ and _bad_ points — so spend some time now _working out_ what you're going to say, and how to _back it up_.

Use the verb Être to talk about your character.

eg   Je suis _sociable/sympathique/gentil(le)/généreux(euse)/amical(e)/travailleur(euse)_
   I am sociable/nice/kind/generous/friendly/hard working

J'ai beaucoup d'amis. Quand ils ont des problèmes je les écoute et je les conseille.
I have a lot of friends. When they have problems I listen to them and give them advice

Don't forget to be a little bit _modest_ — mention some of your _bad points_ too!

Je suis _bavard(e)/paresseux(se)/timide/egoïste/avare/bavard(e) en classe_
I am talkative/lazy/shy/selfish/stingy/talkative in class

Je _n'ai pas beaucoup d'amis_ parce que je ne suis pas facile à vivre.
I don't have many friends because I am difficult to get on with

4) **The Things You Like say a lot about your character**

You can say more about yourself by talking about stuff you like or about your hobbies (see P.45).

eg: J'aime les animaux, j'aime le sport   J'adore les bonbons et les chocolats
      I love animals, I love sport   _I love sweets and chocolates_

Talking about myself — my favourite subject...

Don't forget to say what _kind_ of hair you've got as well as the colour. If you learn the _character_ words, you can sum up your good and bad points and talk about your friends. Brilliant.

More on Your Friends and Family

To get the marks you'll need to be able to talk about _your family_ in more _detail_ — it's boring but you've really got to learn this vocab if you want to pass the Exam.

Extended family — when your distant relatives stretch out

Mon <u>grand-père</u> maternel — My grandfather from my mother's side
Ma <u>grand-mère</u> maternelle — My grandmother from my mother's side
Ils sont tous les deux <u>à la retraite</u> — They are both retired
Ma grand-mère paternelle <u>est morte</u> — My father's mother is dead
Mon grand-père paternel <u>vit avec nous</u> — My father's father lives with us
J'ai deux <u>tantes</u> et trois <u>oncles</u> — I have two aunts and three uncles
J'ai beaucoup de <u>cousins</u> et <u>cousines</u> — I have lots of cousins

Here's the vocab you need to describe a step family:

| beau-père | step father | demi-frère | step/half brother |
| belle-mère | step mother | demi-soeur | step/half sister |

You just can't help being like your Parents

Parfois, j'ai le mauvais caractère de mon père

J'ai les yeux bleus de mon père — I have my father's blue eyes
J'ai le sourire de ma mère — I have my mother's smile
Je suis petit(e) et gentil(le) comme ma mère — I am small and kind like my mother
J'ai le mauvais caractère de mon père — I have my father's bad temper
Parfois je suis critique comme ma mère — Sometimes I am critical like my mother

How to describe stuff you do with your parents

Sometimes you just can't avoid it — your parents want some family bonding time and usually it's chores or shopping (see P.34 and P.73) or maybe holidays (see Section Six), eg:

Je vais toujours en vacances avec mes parents.
I always go on holiday with my parents

Je passe toutes les vacances en famille

How to describe your friends — and still stay friends with them

Mon meilleur ami s'appelle Marc

Mon meilleur ami s'appelle Marc. Il est gentil. Il est grand, il a les cheveux bouclés et il porte des lunettes. Il est drôle et il est très sympathique.
My best friend is called Marc. He is nice. He is tall, he has curly hair and he wears glasses. He is funny and very very nice
Mais je n'aime pas sa petite amie. Je la trouve antipathique, snob et désagréable.
But I don't like his girlfriend. I find her unfriendly, snobbish and nasty

People you like and those you don't — dishing the dirt

J'aime les copains surtout quand ils sont marrants. J'aime les gens intelligents et les gens qui me font rire. Je n'aime pas les gens bêtes et les gens égoïstes.
I like friends particularly when they are funny. I like intelligent people and those who make me laugh. I do not like stupid and selfish people.

I inherited my dress sense — it's my parents' genes...

More lovely vocabulary to help you talk about your nearest and dearest. You need to _learn_ those words and _practise_ them. Remember, it all helps to get you marks at the end of the day.

Daily Routine

The fun never ends here, but this is another of those boring old _Exam favourites_ — so get learning.

1) Get up — and get these verbs learned

Remember your reflexive verbs (see P.16)

Je me réveille tous les jours à sept heures
I get up every day at seven

Je me prépare pour aller à l'école
I get ready for school

Je me lave
I wash myself

Je me brosse les dents
I clean my teeth

Je me coiffe
I comb my hair

Je m'habille
I get dressed

Je fais mon lit et _je range ma chambre_
Vers sept heures trente je vais dans la cuisine
   pour prendre mon _petit déjeuner_
Je mange des céréales et du pain grillé
Je bois du jus de fruit et du thé/du café
À huit heures _je quitte la maison_ pour l'école

I make my bed and tidy my room
Around seven thirty I go in the kitchen
   to have breakfast
I eat cereals and toast
I drink fruit juice and tea/coffee
At eight I leave home for school

2) Saying how you get to school

Je vais à l'école:

à pied	on foot	en voiture	by car
en autobus	by bus	en train	by train

Remember to use "EN" + means of transport EXCEPT FOR à pied

3) Your dead exciting School Routine — Zzzzz

eg: _J'arrive_ à l'école à huit heures et demie
À huit heures quarante-cinq _nous avons une assemblée_
Le premier cours commence à neuf heures.
À onze heures nous avons _une petite récréation_
À une heure moins le quart, nous avons _une pause_
d'une heure pour le _déjeuner_.

I arrive at school at half past eight
At 8.45, _we have assembly_
The first lesson starts at nine
At 11.00 we have _a small break_
At 12.45 we have _one hour break_
for _lunch_

4) The Second Best Part of the Day — Lunch Time

Je déjeune tous les jours à la cantine de l'école. J'aime/je déteste les repas de l'école.
I eat lunch every day at school. I like/hate school dinners.

Il y a une grande choix, et il y a toujours un dessert.
There's lots of choice and there's always a dessert.

Les cours reprennent à deux heures.
Lessons start again at two.

5) The Best Part of the Day

Les cours finissent à quatre heures et je retourne à la maison.
Lessons finish at four o'clock and I go home.

Two good things about school — before it and after it...

Let's face it, your day-in, day-out school routine is _boring_. You can bet there'll be some kind of question about it in the speaking or writing Exams, though. Learn how to say _when_ you do various things — and get all that new _vocabulary_ firmly lodged in the vastness of your brain.

Everyday Activities

Phew — luckily life's not all school, but even _at home_ there are some annoying things to do.

Travaux de ménage — household chores

Use the verb Devoir plus the infinitive to say what you have to do at home

Je dois faire beaucoup de choses à la maison.	_I've got to do a lot of things at home_
Je dois m'occuper de mon petit frère.	_I have to look after my little brother_
Je dois lui donner son goûter.	_I have to give him his tea_
Je dois faire la vaisselle du matin.	_I have to wash the morning's dishes_
À cinq heures je commence à faire mes devoirs.	_At five I start to do my homework_
À six heures ma mère rentre du travail.	_At six my mother comes back from work_

SOME ACE EXAMPLES

Pendant que mon père prépare le dîner, je dois faire le repassage.
Whilst my father gets dinner ready I have to do the ironing

À vingt heures j'aide ma mère à mettre la table.
At eight (pm), I help my mother to lay the table

Puis nous dînons en famille.
Then the family have dinner together

Ma soeur ne fait rien pour aider à la maison.
My sister never does anything to help at home

Quelquefois je passe l'aspirateur.
Sometimes I do the vacuum cleaning

Après le dîner je fais mes devoirs jusqu'à dix heures trente.
After dinner, I do my homework up to ten thirty

Je me couche vers onze heures.
I go to bed at around eleven o'clock

Your weekend routine

Morning routine — le Matin

See Section Four for some excellent vocab on real fun stuff to do at the weekend.

Le samedi je me lève assez tard, vers dix heures.	_On Saturdays I get up quite late, at about ten_
À une heure nous déjeunons.	_We have lunch at one_
Je prends un petit déjeuner copieux, des céréales, des oeufs et du bacon.	_I have a big breakfast, cereal, bacon and eggs_

Those amazingly boring _household chores_ again:

Quelquefois je nettoie la cuisine.	_Sometimes I clean the kitchen_
Pour avoir de l'argent de poche je lave la voiture de mon père.	_I wash my father's car to get pocket money_
Une fois par semaine, je range ma chambre	_Once a week, I tidy my bedroom_
Le samedi j'aide ma mère à faire le ménage.	_On Saturday I help my mother with the house work_

Afternoon routine — l'Après-Midi

L'après-midi, je rencontre mes amis en ville.	_In the afternoon, I meet my friends in town_
Nous faisons les magasins ensemble.	_We go shopping together_
Je passe le dimanche en famille avec mes parents.	_I spend Sundays with my family_

Household activities — excuse me while I die of joy...

Don't worry, you don't have to do all the housework on this page, you've just got to be able to talk about it in French. New words to learn again, so time for the old _cover_ and _scribble_ routine.

Your Local Area

This is a where you can really clean up on the marks — just have a think about your area.

1) Living in Towns and Suburbs

J'habite dans une grande ville au sud-ouest de l'Angleterre / dans la capitale du pays de Galles
I live in a big town in the south west of England / in the capital of Wales

J'habite dans la banlieue de Luton à quinze minutes en voiture/autobus du centre ville.
I live in the suburbs of Luton fifteen minutes by car/bus from the town centre

Use the verb Pouvoir to say what one can do in your town

Dans ma ville on peut: *(In my town one can)*

aller à la patinoire	*go to the ice skating rink*
aller au musée	*go to the museum*

aller au cinéma	*go to the cinema*
aller au théâtre	*go to the theatre*
aller à la piscine	*go to the swimming pool*

Use the expression 'Il y a' to list things that there are in your town

Il y a beaucoup de magasins et de restaurants

eg: Il y a beaucoup de magasins / de restaurants
There are a lot of shops / restaurants

Il y a un centre sportif / des boîtes de nuit
There is a sports centre / some night clubs

Il y a beaucoup de choses intéressantes à faire
There are a lot of interesting things to do

If you like living in town, here's what you can say

J'aime beaucoup habiter en ville
I like living in town

Je suis toujours au courant
I always know what's going on

C'est facile pour rencontrer ses amis
It's easy to meet one's friends

C'est très pratique pour aller partout
It's very practical for going everywhere

If you don't like living in town, here are the reasons you can give

Je n'aime pas habiter en ville
I don't like living in town

L'air est trop pollué et les gens jettent leurs déchets partout
The air is too polluted and people throw their rubbish everywhere

Il y a trop de bruit / trop de circulation / trop de monde
There is too much noise / too much traffic / too many people

2) Living in the Country

J'habite à la campagne. C'est très tranquille et il y a beaucoup de champs
I live in the country. It's very peaceful and there are a lot of fields
Nous avons beaucoup d'animaux et j'adore les animaux
We have lots of animals and I love animals
J'adore l'équitation et je peux en faire beaucoup à la campagne
I love horseriding and I can do a lot of it in the country

If you don't like living there use Pouvoir and the expression 'Il y a' in the negative

Je ne peux pas voir mes amis souvent et il n'y a rien à faire là où j'habite.
I can't see my friends often and there's nothing to do where I live

NOTE: Practise your negatives by <u>changing</u> all the positive sentences on this page to say the <u>opposite</u> — it won't cheer you up but it'll help you revise your <u>negative phrases</u>.

Describing Your Home

One way to show off your French skills <u>without</u> too much work is to learn how to talk about your <u>home</u> — just scribble a list of the <u>helpful vocab</u> on the page, work out translations and <u>get learning</u>.

What <u>type of house/home</u> you have and <u>where it is</u>

1) J'habite une petite maison dans la banlieue de Londres.
I live in a small house in a suburb of London.
Nous avons trois chambres à coucher, un salon, une salle à manger, une cuisine et une salle de bains.
We have three bedrooms, a living room, a dining room, a kitchen and a bathroom.
C'est une vieille maison et j'y habite depuis cinq ans.
It's an old house and I've lived there for five years.

2) J'habite une grande maison en pleine campagne. C'est une maison en briques et c'est une maison moderne. C'est une maison à deux étages.
I live in a large house in the country. It's a house made of bricks and it is a modern house. It's a two-storey house.
Nous avons dix pièces, y compris quatre chambres, un salon, une grande cuisine, deux salles de bains et un bureau. Nous avons aussi un grand garage et un jardin.
We have ten rooms, including four bedrooms, a living room, a large kitchen, two bathrooms and a study. We've also a garage and a garden.

3) J'habite un appartement en plein centre ville et j'aime beaucoup ça.
I live in an apartment in the town centre and I love it.

Talking about Your Room

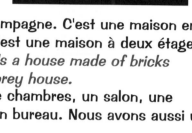

Ma chambre est située au premier étage.
My room is on the first floor.

C'est une grande chambre avec une vue superbe sur les collines.
It's a big room with a superb view of the hills.

Dans ma chambre, il y a un lit, une armoire, un fauteuil, et une table de travail.
In my bedroom there is a bed, a wardrobe, an armchair and a writing desk.

J'ai une chaîne hi-fi dans ma chambre et beaucoup de disques compacts et de livres.
I have a hi-fi system and lots of CDs and books.

J'ai ma propre chambre / je partage une chambre avec ma soeur/mon frère.
I have my own room / I share with my sister/brother.

The best of the rest — some other rooms

Dans un coin du salon se trouve le piano et dans l'autre coin, la télévision.
In one corner of the room is the piano and in the other the television.

J'aime beaucoup notre salon. Il y a des peintures au mur et des meubles anciens.
I like our living room very much. There are some paintings and some old furniture.

Au rez-de-chaussée se trouvent le salon, la salle à manger, la cuisine et le bureau.
On the ground floor are the living room, the dining room, the kitchen and the study.

Loads of Homes — but no Watson...

Being able to describe where you live and what your house is like is going to be very useful for the writing and speaking Exams. You need to learn <u>how</u> to describe a place and the new <u>words</u> to describe it with. <u>Cover</u>, <u>scribble</u> and <u>learn</u>, and one day those marks will be yours.

Being Polite to Hosts and Guests

Being polite is dead useful for _role-plays_ — if you have to pretend you're on a French exchange or you've got a French person visiting. Learn this lot so you can be charming _and_ get top marks.

1) _Asking Permission — Remember to be Polite_

Remember to use Est-ce que + je + Pouvoir in the present + Infinitive

a) Use the phone to speak to your parents   _Est-ce que je peux téléphoner à mes parents SVP?_

b) Ask for a towel as you've forgotten to bring one   _Est-ce que je peux avoir une serviette s'il vous plaît? J'ai oublié d'en apporter une._

c) Watch TV   _Est-ce que je peux regarder la télévision s'il vous plaît?_

d) Have a bath   _Est-ce que je peux prendre un bain s'il vous plaît?_

e) Go to bed   _Est-ce que je peux aller dormir s'il vous plaît?_

Remember that you need to address your penfriend's parents as Vous and him/her as Tu

2) _Asking a Visitor what they want to do_

Change 'je peux' into 'tu voudrais' and the possessive adjective into the 2ⁿᵈ person (mon into ton) without the SVP.

eg: Est-ce que tu voudrais téléphoner à tes parents?

a) Going out   Est-ce que tu voudrais sortir?

b) Go to the cinema   Est-ce que tu voudrais aller au cinéma?

c) Have a game of tennis/chess   Est-ce que tu voudrais jouer au tennis/aux échecs?

3) _Saying Sorry — and sounding like you mean it_

eg: _Je suis désolé(e)_ mais je ne mange pas de viande. Je suis végétarien(ne).
I'm sorry but I don't eat meat. I'm a vegetarian.

Excusez-moi mais je ne me sens pas bien, je voudrais voir un médecin.
I don't feel well, I'd like to see a doctor.

Je suis désolé(e), mais je n'ai pas faim.
I'm sorry, but I'm not hungry.

Excusez-moi, mais j'ai cassé un verre.
I'm sorry, but I've broken a glass.

4) _How to offer to help in the house_

It may sound like sucking up, but it's a good way of showing the examiner you know how to form _questions_ — and it'll get you _extra marks_: **Est-ce que je peux vous aider+ à + infinitive**

eg: Est-ce que je peux vous aider à faire la vaisselle?   _Can I help you with the washing up?_
Est-ce que je peux vous aider à faire la cuisine?   _Can I help you in the kitchen?_
Est-ce que je peux vous aider à mettre la table?   _Can I help you to lay the table?_

5) _How to thank your hosts at the end of your stay_

Je vous remercie de votre hospitalité.   _Thank you for your hospitality._

Hospitality — your guest is as good as mine...

Being polite isn't only useful for real life, it can get you more _marks_ in the _Exams_, too. _Learn_ those polite little phrases on this page. The bit about offering to help doesn't mean that you should offer to do the examiner's washing up in return for a better grade, you know...

Revision Summary for Section Two

Loads to learn in this section — and these brilliant test-yourself revision questions are just the job for practising. The best way to make sure you've got it all sorted is to practise — answers to be given in French of course. This is all important basic stuff for the Exam so you need to know it backwards. But start by working through these questions to see how well you do. Then go over the tricky bits again. Take the time now to think up good answers and practise the best ways of saying different things. You'll get more marks for using interesting vocabulary — but only if you use it accurately. So learn it the right way. And remember — keep at it. It's the only way to stay on top of things.

1) What nationality are you? Where were you born? Give full sentence answers.
2) When is your birthday?
3) How would you ask your French penpal where he/she lives?
4) Describe your parents. Give four facts about them.
5) Do you have brothers and sisters? Do you get on with them?
6) Do you have any pets? Describe three features of a pet you have or one you would like.
7) Describe two of your friends, giving three features of each.
8) Give five facts about your own physical appearance and five facts about your character.
9) What do you and your friends like to do for fun?
10) What are your good points and what are your bad points?
11) Leo has just seen Kate in the street and he has fallen in love with her. He writes her a letter telling her about himself. How would he say he is: a) blond b) blue-eyed c) slim d) friendly?
12) Kate writes a note back to Leo. How would she say she likes: a) cakes b) action films c) boybands d) going to the gym?
13) Zeke is visiting from Alabama in the USA. He tells his French penfriend all about his family. How would he say he lives with his grandmother on his mother's side, his two half-sisters and his four cousins? How would he say his paternal grandfather lives with them?
14) Describe two traits you think you have inherited from your parents.
15) Write a short paragraph describing your best friend.
16) Describe your morning routine. Give five things that you do before going to school.
17) How do you get to school every day?
18) Write a short paragraph describing your lunch hour.
19) List all the household chores you do. Do you like doing them?
20) What do you do at the weekend? Give at least four different things.
21) Describe exactly where you live. Do you like it?
22) Give two good and two bad features about where you live.
23) What kind of house do you live in? Describe all the rooms.
24) How would you ask permission to have a shower?
25) Kate is visiting Leo. How would he ask her if she wants to make a phone call?
26) Leo has made Kate a black pudding, egg and lard sandwich. How does Kate say she's sorry but she doesn't eat meat because she's vegetarian? How does she say she feels sick?
27) How would you ask to help: a) wash up b) lay the table c) cook the dinner?
28) What do you do when you've finished school for the day?
29) Catherine is showing you her stamp collection and you find this really boring. How would you suggest going to the swimming pool?
30) How do you thank your hosts for their hospitality?

Classroom Objects and School Subjects

I don't believe it — more dull _school stuff_, but this is dead important for getting _top Exam marks_.

La Salle de Classe — The Classroom

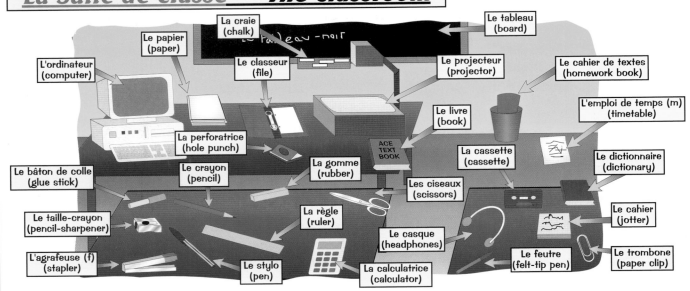

La craie (chalk)
Le tableau (board)
Le papier (paper)
L'ordinateur (computer)
Le classeur (file)
Le projecteur (projector)
Le cahier de textes (homework book)
Le livre (book)
L'emploi de temps (m) (timetable)
La perforatrice (hole punch)
ACE TEXT BOOK
La cassette (cassette)
Le dictionnaire (dictionary)
Le bâton de colle (glue stick)
Le crayon (pencil)
La gomme (rubber)
Les ciseaux (scissors)
Le taille-crayon (pencil-sharpener)
La règle (ruler)
Le cahier (jotter)
L'agrafeuse (f) (stapler)
Le casque (headphones)
Le feutre (felt-tip pen)
Le trombone (paper clip)
Le stylo (pen)
La calculatrice (calculator)

Les Matières — School Subjects

Spend some time learning this vocab so you'll have plenty to talk and write about in the Exam:

l'anglais (m)	_English_
les maths (f)	_maths_
l'histoire (f)	_history_
les langues (f)	_languages_
le français	_French_
l'allemand	_German_
l'espagnol	_Spanish_
l'italien	_Italian_

la géographie	_geography_
le dessin	_art_
EMT (enseignement manuel et technique)	_craft, design and technology_
les sciences naturelles (f pl)	_science_
la physique	_physics_
la chimie	_chemistry_
la biologie	_biology_

les études ménagères	_home economics_
l'informatique	_computing studies_
les études contemporaines	_modern studies_
l'instruction civique (f)	_social studies_
l'instruction réligieuse	_religious studies_
l'éducation physique	_physical education_
la musique	_music_
le commerce	_business studies_
les études de secrétairiat (fpl)	_secretarial studies_
l'électronique (f)	_electronics_

Classroom Expressions

OK, I know this is boring but this stuff is basic French — and it's a great way of practising for your <u>Oral Exam</u>. Make sure you understand how to form instructions and talk about problems.

Instructions — those Amazing Imperatives again

Right — start by going back and checking over P.22 on Imperatives. Then have a look at these.

1) Instructions to One Person

tu form of the verb

(take off the *S* with *ER* verbs)

eg: répète!   *repeat!*
finis!   *finish!*
attends!   *wait!*

2) Instructions to Two or More People

vous form of the verb

eg: fermez les cahiers!   *close the jotters!*
ouvrez les fenêtres!   *open the windows!*
prenez vos livres!   *take your books!*

3) For Negative Instructions

ne + verb + pas

eg: ne triche *pas!*   *don't cheat!*
ne copie *pas!*   *don't copy!*

4) With Reflexives

verb + dash + emphatic pronoun

lève-*toi!*   *stand up!*   levez-*vous!*   *stand up!*
assieds-*toi!*   *sit down!*   asseyez-*vous!*   *sit down!*
tais-*toi!*   *be quiet!*   taisez-*vous!*   *be quiet!*

5) With Negative Reflexives

ne + reflexive pronoun + verb + pas

ne *te* lève pas!   *don't stand up!*
ne *vous* levez pas!   *don't stand up!*
ne *t'*assieds pas!   *don't sit down!*

Those Minor School Problems in Full

You need to know how to make <u>excuses</u> in French — and not just for School role-plays:

ne + avoir + pas + de

(means *you don't have something*)

Other Useful Phrases:

J'ai <u>oublié</u> mon cahier   *I have <u>forgotten</u> my jotter*
J'ai <u>perdu</u> ma trousse   *I have <u>lost</u> my pencil case*

<u>Je peux avoir</u> une feuille de papier?   <u>May I have</u> a piece of paper?
<u>Je peux emprunter</u> un crayon?   <u>May I borrow</u> a pencil?

Learn your imperatives — this page will self-instruct...

This is the <u>imperative</u>. You've seen it in the grammar section and now here it is at work. As well as the grammar stuff, there's some new <u>vocabulary</u> for things like losing your jotter, borrowing a pen and copying from each other. All there to be <u>learned</u>, and what's more, <u>remembered</u>.

Your School and School Routine

They just won't let it lie... Those examiners are obsessed with _school vocab_ — so learn it now.

Some Different Types of School

The French equivalent of a comprehensive is "_un collège d'enseignement secondaire_" or _CES_.
Most of the time you'd simply say "_un collège mixte_" (a mixed secondary school). "_Un lycée_" is
a French sixth-form college. "_Une école privée_" (a private school) is less common in France.

To say that you go to a certain type of school use: **aller + à + type of school**

eg: Je vais à un collège mixte _I go to a mixed comprehensive school_

Year Groups

The French year group equivalents go the _reverse order_ from our numbering system.

To say which class you or a friend are in use:

être + en + class

eg: Je suis _en_ seconde
I'm in the fifth year/S5/Year 11

Mon copain est _en_ terminale
My friend is in the upper sixth

French year group	English year group
en sixième	in the first year
en cinquième	in the second year
en quatrième	in the third year
en troisième	in the fourth year
en seconde	in the fifth year
en première	in the lower sixth
en terminale	in the upper sixth

Describing the School Building

Here is a group of adjectives/adverbs you'll find useful for describing the building — politely that is.

assez	quite/fairly	en béton	concrete
tout à fait	completely	en bois	wood/wooden
un peu	a bit	en brique	brick
moderne	modern	en pierre	stone

Le collège est très moderne!

eg: mon collège est........un grand bâtiment _en brique_.
My school is a large brick building
mon collège a ....deux bâtiments _modernes_.
My school has two modern buildings

Those Rivetingly Exciting School Rooms/Areas

un laboratoire	laboratory	la salle de classe	classroom	le foyer des élèves	common room
la cantine	canteen	la bibliothèque	library	au rez-de-chaussée	on the ground floor
un atelier	workshop	la salle de gym	gymnasium	au deuxième étage	on the second floor
la cour	playground	le terrain de sports	sportsground	au premier étage	on the first floor

Talking about your School Routine

Le jour scolaire commence/finit à...
The school day begins/ends at .....
Le professeur fait l'appel
The teacher does the register
Les cours commencent à + time
Lessons begin at ......
Chaque cours dure + number + minutes
Each lesson lasts .... minutes
Il y a une récréation
There's a break

L'heure du déjeuner est à + time
Lunch hour is at ....
J'ai huit cours par jour
I have 8 lessons per day
On peut manger dans la cantine
You can eat in the canteen
Samedi est un jour de congé
Saturday is a holiday
La rentrée est au mois de septembre
The school year starts in September

Je dois porter un uniforme
I have to wear a uniform
Le trimestre
the term
Je vais au collège
à pied/en vélo
I walk/cycle to school
Nous y allons
en auto/en bus
We go by car/by bus

School — mi favrít clas is speling...

Remember, you need to know the names of the different _types_ of school. Don't forget the
phrases for your exciting school _routine_ and the names of your wild and windswept _classrooms_.

Opinions About School

Time for some opinions — what do you really think. Don't hold back — but do use good French.

1) Some Adjectives to describe your Strengths and Weaknesses

fort(e)	good	faible	weak
moyen(ne)	average	nul(le)	hopeless

To talk about how you or a friend feel about a subject:

être + strength/weakness + en + subject

eg: Je suis *fort(e)* *en* anglais — *I am good at English*
Sara est *nulle* *en* dessin — *Sara is hopeless at art*

2) Your Favourite and Least Favourite Subjects

1) This is where you can have a little fun — but remember to give your *reasons*:

ma matière *préférée est* / *préférées sont*... — *my favourite subject is / subjects are...*
je *n'aime pas* / je *déteste*... — *I don't like / hate...*

2) To state your reason for liking or disliking a subject use:

c'est (it is) + adjective

It'll really help to learn these smashing adjectives:

facile	easy	difficile	difficult
barbant(e)	boring	intéressant(e)	interesting
chouette	great	super	great
drôle	funny	compliqué(e)	complicated

Ma matière préférée est le français, c'est *chouette*.
My favourite subject is French, it's great
Je déteste la chimie, c'est *compliquée*.
I hate chemistry, it's complicated

3) Saying what you think about your Teachers...but carefully

To say you've got a favourite teacher: Mon prof(esseur) préféré est ...
To say you dislike a particular teacher: Je n'aime pas le prof de + subject

J'aime le prof de français

And don't just say whether you do or don't like them, say why:

sévère	strict	grave	serious
marrant(e)	funny	excellent(e)	excellent
ennuyeux(euse)	boring	gentil(le)	nice
sympa	nice	travailleur(euse)	hard-working
aimable	pleasant	désagréable	unpleasant

Make a whole sentence and join the bits with '*parce que*' (because)

eg: J'aime le prof de maths *parce qu*'il est sympa. — *I like the maths teacher because he is nice*

4) Talking about Exams and Results — just what you need

J'ai réussi!

Je vais passer mes examens cette année — *I'm going to sit my exams this year*
J'ai réussi à mon examen de + subject — *I passed my exam in...*
J'ai de bonnes/mauvaises notes — *I get good/bad marks*
J'ai raté mon examen de + subject — *I failed my exam in...*
Je voudrais continuer mes études — *I would like to continue my studies*
Je vais étudier + subject — *I am going to study...*

I hate Exams — the teachers get all testy...

Shed-loads of top-class adjectives for you to use and learn. You can say whether you're good at a subject and why you like a particular teacher or lesson. Don't forget, *passer un examen* is to *sit* an exam, *not* to *pass* it. Lots of new vocabulary here, so cover, scribble and *learn*.

Revision Summary for Section Three

School's out — but this is where the learning really starts. It's that spiffingly super revision summary time again — just what you need to test those aching brains. Yes it's a pain, but you've really got to do it now... if you want to get the marks in the Exam. Talking about school can be pretty boring, but there are loads of easy marks here if you learn those descriptive words and phrases properly. So start by working through these questions — and don't worry if you get stuck. Just keep going over the section till you can get every single one of these juicy questions completely and utterly right. So come on then.

1) Give the names in French of ten important items that you would find in a classroom.
2) Make a list of the names of 15 different school subjects in French. Then make a list of all the subjects that you study at school.
3) How do you give instructions in French: a) to one person b) to two or more people c) for negative instructions d) with reflexive verbs?
4) Give two examples of each kind of instruction in the last question.
5) Someone has dangerously put glue on the chairs in the French classroom. How would the teacher instruct her students not to sit down?
6) Today there is a French test. How would you say that you don't have your pen?
7) There's a school swimming competition at the local leisure centre today, but the pool looks really cold. How would you say you forgot your swimming costume (le maillot de bain)?
8) How could you ask to borrow a football instead?
9) Kate is listening to the new album by the Condiment Boyz, but Leo is talking too loudly for her to hear it properly. How does Kate tell him to be quiet?
10) What is the French equivalent of: a) a comprehensive b) a sixth-form college c) a private school d) a mixed school?
11) What is the difference between French year group numbers and the British system?
12) Describe your school building using five different phrases.
13) Name four school rooms and describe where they are found in the building or grounds of your school.
14) Write a paragraph describing your daily school routine using at least eight different phrases.
15) Describe whether you are strong or weak in two different subjects.
16) Which is your favourite subject at school? Explain why, giving at least two reasons.
17) Which is your least favourite subject? Explain why, and give three reasons.
18) Name two more subjects you don't like, and give a reason in each case.
19) Give the names of three teachers you dislike, and explain why (remember to think up good reasons for the Exams, or you won't pick up the marks).
20) Name one teacher you like and explain why.
21) How would you say you are going to take your exams this year?
22) Say whether you would like to continue your studies in the future.
23) Say whether or not you like school.
24) Say what your favourite part of the school day is.
25) Do you like school dinners? If so, why?

Hobbies

Yep — it's hobby time. This is dead easy really — you just have to talk about what you *like to do*.

Saying What Hobbies You Have

Je fais + du/de la/de l'/des + noun

Je vais + au/à la/à l'/aux + noun

Je regarde + un/une/le/la + noun

J'écoute + le/la/les + noun

Je lis + un/une/les + noun

Je joue + au/à la/à l'/aux + noun

> **REMEMBER:** — **Je fais** comes from **FAIRE**
> — **Je vais** comes from **ALLER**
> — **Je lis** comes from **LIRE**

> *FAIRE* is used in many expressions where it *changes its meaning*. You need to learn which expressions use *FAIRE*, which use *ALLER* and which use *OTHER VERBS*.

Expressing Opinions About Hobbies

There are *four top verbs* you can use to *express your opinion* about hobbies:

PRÉFÉRER	— Je préfère..........	*to prefer*
AIMER	— J'aime..............	*to like*
DÉTESTER	— Je déteste........	*to hate*
ADORER	— J'adore.............	*to adore*

eg: Je *préfère* jouer au football *I prefer playing football*
Je *préfère* le football *I prefer football*

You can replace
Je préfère **with:**

J'aime	*I like*
Je déteste	*I hate*
J'adore	*I adore*

Explaining why you like something — Parce que...

Use: **Parce que + c'est + adjective** or **À mon avis + c'est + adjective**

(Because it's........) (In my opinion it's.....)

eg: *Pourquoi* aimes-tu la gymnastique? *Why do you like gymnastics?*

> **REMEMBER:**
> **Pourquoi? = Why?**

J'aime la gymnastique *parce que* c'est amusant. *À mon avis* c'est intéressant.

I like gymnastics because it's fun *In my opinion it's interesting*

Asking Someone Else About Their Hobbies

Use: **Qu'est-ce que tu préfères faire?** **Comment passes-tu tes heures libres?**

(What do you prefer to do?) (How do you spend your free time?)

I love football — it's kicking...

A whole page on those wonderful exciting things that you get up to outside school. Learn all the ways of saying what you *do*, what you *watch* and what you *play*. The rest of the page takes you up to the heady heights of actually saying *why* you like the things you do.

Interests and Activities

OK — time for your _top three activity verbs_ — faire, aller and jouer. Make sure you learn _which activities_ go with _which verb_ — and don't get confused. There's loads to do here so get cracking.

Faire — to Do, to Make, to Go etc

Je _fais des_ promenades	I go for walks
Je _fais de la_ gymnastique	I do gymnastics
Je _fais de la_ photo	I do photography
Je _fais du_ vélo	I go cycling

Aller — to Go

Je _vais au_ cinéma	I go to the cinema
Je _vais au_ concert	I go to the concert
Je _vais au_ centre des jeunes	I go to the youth club
Je _vais à la_ discothèque	I go to the disco
Je _vais à la_ boîte de nuit	I go to the nightclub

Je _vais à la_ pêche	I go fishing
Je _vais au_ match de football	I go to the football match
Je _vais à la_ surprise-partie	I go to the party
Je _vais au_ théâtre	I go to the theatre

Jouer — to Play

Je _joue aux_ cartes	Je _joue au_ football	Je _joue avec_ mon ordinateur
I play cards	I play football	I play on my computer

Jouer is _normally_ followed by au/à la/à l'/aux + noun. _BUT_ if you want to say "_I play_" followed by a _musical instrument_, you have to use du/de la/de l'/des.

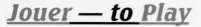

Je joue + du/de la/de l'/des + musical instrument

eg:	Je joue _du_ piano	I play the piano
	Je joue _de la_ guitare	I play the guitar

Other Verbs used for things you do

Je _regarde un_ film	I watch a film	Je _lis un_ livre	I read a book
Je _regarde la_ télévision	I watch the television	Je _lis un_ magazine	I read a magazine

Un film d'amour (romance film)	Un film d'aventures (adventure film)	Un film policier (detective film)	Un film comique (comedy film)	Un film d'épouvante (horror film)

J'_écoute un_ disque compact	J'_écoute de_ la musique	J'_écoute la_ radio
I listen to a CD	I listen to music	I listen to the radio

Verbs — they're where the action is...

You've got _activities_, you're gonna need _verbs_. Think about it — it stands to reason. Learn what things you can do, make, go to and play, and don't forget to use the je form of these verbs.

Sports

Saying *What Sports* You Play

Je joue + au/à la/à l'/aux + sport	Je fais + du/de la/de l'/des + sport
(I play + sport)	(I do + sport)

Je joue au ...

foot

rugby

tennis

golf

volley

tennis de table

basket-ball

hockey (sur glace)

cricket

Je joue aux ...

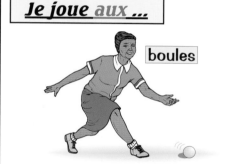

boules

Je fais de l' ...

alpinisme

escrime

Je fais du ...

ski

vélo

ski nautique

patinage

Je fais de la ...

gymnastique

voile

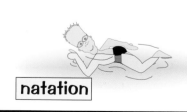

natation

planche à voile

Revising sport — they think it's all over...

All lovely stuff about doing sport and being wonderfully fit and healthy, and a page full of nice pictures, too. Don't forget that the point here is to get sorted in your mind *which* sports use jouer *au*, faire *du*, faire *de la* etc. Cover, scribble, learn and enjoy.

Talking about Sports

Sports could come up anywhere in the Exam, but it's particularly good for talking or writing about yourself.

1) Saying *Where* you *Play* Sports

Je joue + au/à la/à l'/aux + sport + place

eg:
au stade	*at the stadium*
au club des jeunes	*at the youth club*
dans le gymnase	*in the gymnasium*
au jardin public	*in the park*
à la piscine	*at the swimming pool*
à la montagne	*in the mountains*
à la plage	*at the beach*

2) Saying you *Watch* Sports on *TV*

Je regarde + le/la/les + sport + à la télévision

(I watch + sport + on television)

Remind yourself of the days of the week on P.27 so that you can say when you watch sport on TV

Je regarde le football à la télé le samedi soir
I watch football on TV on Saturday evenings

3) *Expressing Opinions* About Sport

sport + est + adjective

La natation est amusante!

eg: Le tennis est amusant
Tennis is fun

REMEMBER that *adjectives* have to *agree* with the noun they're describing

La natation est amusan*t*e
Swimming is fun

<u>NOTE:</u> Look back to P.46 for other ways of expressing opinions.
Use the adjectives you've learnt in other sections to talk about sports.

4) *Sports and Seasons*

Use: **season + je joue/je fais + sport**

les saisons	the seasons
au printemps	in spring
en été	in summer
en automne	in autumn
en hiver	in winter

En hiver je fais du ski
In winter I go skiing

En été je joue au tennis
In summer I play tennis

Be a sport — what's French for a game of two halves...

More sport vocabulary, this time mixed in with a good portion of grammar. The two tricky bits are remembering if the <u>place</u> you do your sport is masculine or feminine so you get your <u>au</u> and <u>à la</u> right, and remembering whether the <u>sport itself</u> is masculine or feminine so that any adjective you're using will <u>agree</u>. Scribble a quick paragraph with three details about your favourite sport.

Deciding to Go Out

This could come up anywhere in the Exam, particularly in the _Oral_ or the _Listening_ — so learn it now.

Making Suggestions — _si on + imperfect_

There are loads of ways to suggest doing something — and in French you'll sound dead charming:

Use: **si on + verb in the imperfect + time/day/date?**

Look back at P.20 to remind yourself how to form the imperfect tense.

1) _Si on Allait_ — Shall we Go...

au théâtre?

au club?
CLUB

à la boum
à la surprise-partie

au cinéma

2) _Si on Faisait_ — Shall we...

une promenade?
go for a walk?

une promenade à la campagne
a walk in the country

une promenade à la montagne
a walk in the mountains

Making Suggestions _Using VOULOIR_

Use: **Voulez-vous + infinitive** or **Veux-tu + infinitive**

eg: _Voulez-vous_ aller au cinéma ce soir?   _Do you want to go to the cinema tonight?_
     Veux-tu aller danser demain soir?   _Do you want to go dancing tomorrow night?_

> **REMEMBER:** — Use 'tu' when speaking to one person you're _friendly_ with
>   or _the same age as_.
>   — Use 'vous' when speaking to one person to whom you must
>   be _polite_, or when speaking to _more than one person_.

eg: Papa, _tu_ veux aller au parc?   _Do you want to go to the park, dad?_
     Monsieur, voulez-_vous_ dîner au restaurant? _Would you like to dine in the restaurant, sir?_
     Pierre et Anne, voulez-_vous_ chanter?   _Peter and Anne, do you want to sing?_

Voulez-vous — isn't that something to do with ABBA...

All good useful stuff. It's worth having a look back at the grammar section to remind you how to form the _imperfect_ tense. Don't be confused by using the imperfect when you're actually talking about the future — it's like they're saying "what if we _went_ to the park", you see.

Arranging to Meet

This page is all about going out on the town — provided you can meet up with your friends first...

Arranging The Meeting Place

Si on se rencontrait au/à la/à l'/chez + place
= Let's meet up at....

Rendez-vous au/à la/à l'/chez + place
= Meet up at...

au café

CAFÉ

at the cafe

à la poste

Poste

at the post office

à l'hôtel de ville

at the town hall

SI ON SE RENCONTRAIT...?
(Let's meet)

chez moi

at my place

chez toi

at your place

chez Patricia

at Patricia's place

Giving a Time to meet

Use:

ce soir

1st

this evening

demain (soir)

2nd

tomorrow (evening)

après-demain (soir)

3rd

the day after tomorrow (evening)

à huit heures

at eight o'clock

Saying Exactly Where

Use:

derrière	=	behind
devant	=	in front of
en face de	=	opposite
à droite de	=	to the right of
à gauche de	=	to the left of
à côté de	=	next to

à côté de (next to)

Derrière (behind)

à gauche de (to the left of)

à droite de (to the right of)

Devant (in front of)

En face de (opposite)

eg:
Rendez-vous *derrière* la gare
Si on se rencontrait *devant* la poste
Rendez-vous *à gauche du* cinéma

We'll meet behind the station
Let's meet in front of the post office
We'll meet at the left of the cinema

Going out with someone — don't get your dates wrong...

Three nice *easy* bits to this page. *Where*, *when* and *exactly* where. No point in Kate kicking her heels at the back of the town hall if Leo's standing at the front of the town hall with a red carnation in his lapel and a box of chocolates. Make sure you learn all the vocab carefully.

Out on the Town

So when you're on the town you'll need to know how to _get tickets_ for shows — or better still, make sure you learn how to book them _in advance_. This is another Exam favourite — get learning.

Buying Tickets — _Les Billets_

Je voudrais + number + billet(s)/place(s) + type

un billet enfant	_one child ticket_
deux places adultes	_two adult seats_
un billet demi-tarif	_a half-price ticket_
un billet étudiant	_a student ticket_
une place réduite	_a reduced-price seat_

Saying _Which Performance_

La séance de + time or **La première/dernière séance**

eg: Deux billets étudiants pour _la première séance_ s'il vous plaît.
Two student tickets for the first showing please

Un billet adulte pour _la dernière séance_ s'il vous plaît.
One adult ticket for the last showing please

Trois places enfants pour _la séance de neuf heures_.
Three child's seats for the nine o'clock showing

ça commence à neuf heures

Asking _About_ Times — _À quelle heure commence/finit?_

Once you know what's on, it's best to find out when the show ends — especially if you need to get home on the bus afterwards.

LE MONSTRE

à huit heures

eg: À quelle heure _commence_ Le Monstre?
When does The Monster begin?

Ça _commence_ à huit heures.
It starts at eight

Ça finit à dix heures et quart

À quelle heure _finit_ le spectacle?
When does the show end?
Ça _finit_ à dix heures et quart.
It finishes at quarter past ten

Do I need to _reserve_ seats? — _Il faut réserver_ + time?

eg: _Il faut réserver_ pour demain/samedi?   _Il faut réserver_ pour la séance de huit heures?
Do I need to book for tomorrow/Saturday? _Do I need to book for the eight o'clock performance?_

That show is all too much for me — I can't afford it...

Phew — just a little bit of new _vocabulary_ to stimulate your brain cells, and a couple of jolly pictures to help it along. Don't forget how to say _which_ showing you want the tickets for and how to ask _when_ it starts or finishes. You must make sure you've got all this vocab sorted.

Invitations and Pocket Money

We've covered arranging to meet up and going out, but here's what happens when you just have to say no — and you want to be as polite as you can. There's also some vocab for preferences.

Accepting or Rejecting an Invitation

Use:

> **Je veux bien + expression of acceptance**
> (I'd really like to.......)
>
> or
>
> **Je ne peux pas + expression of regret**
> (I can't.......)

Certainement

Bonne idée!

C'est chouette

JE VEUX BIEN

Avec plaisir

D'accord!

Bien sûr

JE NE PEUX PAS

je m'excuse

malheureusement

Je regrette

Je suis désolée

C'est impossible

Parce que je travaille

Zut!!

Preferences and Alternatives

If you say no to one thing you must suggest something else:

Ça t'intéresse + noun?	(Do you fancy...?)
Non, je préfère + noun.	(No, I prefer...)

Ça t'intéresse, la boum? *Do you fancy the party?*

Non, je préfère le cinéma. *No, I prefer the cinema.*

Pocket Money — Argent de Poche

Unfortunately you've got to pay for all this going out somehow — either with your allowance or any wages you earn from part-time work:

> **Je reçois/gagne + amount + how often**

eg: *Je reçois/gagne* dix livres sterling   *I get/earn ten pounds*

par semaine *per week*   par jour *per day*

par mois *per month*   par heure *per hour* (yeah right)

J'économise cinq livres   *I save five pounds*

Money makes the world go round — if it buys a motor...

Two subjects squished onto one page — but both really important. If you get a role play on _going out_ in the Oral Exam you may have to _turn down_ an invitation, or _suggest_ something else instead.

Revision Summary for Section Four

And now your favourite bit — some more smashing revision questions. It's the only way...
Make sure you get these answers sorted and keep on going over the questions again and again.
This is a really important topic for the Exam — if you learn this stuff well you can pick up loads
of massively valuable marks. Remember — answer the following questions in French and in full
sentences with as much detail as you can give. It's the best way to see what you know.

1) Name three different hobbies you have, using three different verbs.
2) Say which of the three you like most and explain why.
3) List three hobbies people have that you hate. Give reasons why you dislike them.
4) How would you ask a French student what he/she does in his/her spare time?
5) Kate is a massive fan of the boyband the Condiment Boyz, but Leo prefers the rock group the Microhards. How would Kate say that she likes the Condiment Boyz? How would she say she prefers them to the Microhards? How would Leo say that in his opinion the Microhards are better because they can play their instruments and write good songs?
6) Give a list of the five key verbs you need to know for talking about hobbies.
7) How would you say that you: a) go to the cinema every weekend b) watch a film c) play on the computer d) go to the nightclub e) play the guitar?
8) List two sports that take the verb jouer and two that take the verb faire. What preposition does each verb take? Give three examples of sentences using each verb.
9) How would you say that you: a) go fencing b) play cricket c) play ice hockey?
10) Where do people: a) go swimming b) play football? Give two answers for each.
11) What is your favourite sport and why? What is your least favourite and why?
12) Give two sports you can play in: a) winter b) summer c) spring.
13) How would you arrange with a friend to go: a) to the theatre b) to the cinema c) for a walk in the country?
14) Leo wants to ask Kate if she'd like to go dancing tomorrow night, but he is a little bit nervous. How would he ask her out?
15) Kate wants to see a film with a big group of friends instead. How would she ask them if they want to go to the cinema tomorrow?
16) Kate's friends said no, so she decided to go dancing with Leo after all. How would Leo arrange to meet Kate in front of the Town Hall, tomorrow evening at 9.30?
17) How would you ask for three adult seats and two student tickets for the concert?
18) How would you ask for reduced price tickets for the last showing at the cinema? Ask what time the film begins.
19) How would you ask to reserve two tickets for Saturday's performance of Romeo and Juliet, starting at eight o'clock?
20) A friend invites you to see a film. How would you accept and say you really want to go?
21) How would you say you'd prefer to go to the party?
22) How would you say you can't go because you've got too much homework?
23) How much pocket money do you get? What do you spend it on?
24) Comment passes-tu tes heures libres? Que fais-tu le weekend?
25) Quelle sorte de film préfères-tu?
26) Quel genre de musique préfères-tu?
27) Tu regardes la télévision souvent?
28) Est-ce que tu aimes le football? Pourquoi/pourquoi pas?
29) Tu regardes les sports à la télévision?
30) Tu pratiques quels sports en été?

Food Vocabulary

Where would we be without food...Hungry probably. This is a key topic — make sure you understand all about _restaurants_ for role-plays. But first, let's talk about _kinds of food_.

Les Légumes — **Vegetables (don't you just love them!)**

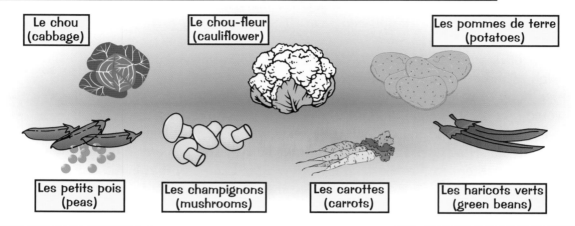

Le chou (cabbage)   **Le chou-fleur** (cauliflower)   **Les pommes de terre** (potatoes)

Les petits pois (peas)   **Les champignons** (mushrooms)   **Les carottes** (carrots)   **Les haricots verts** (green beans)

Les Fruits — **Fruit**

Les Entrées — **Starters**

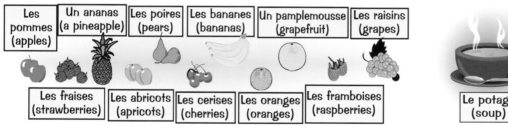

Les pommes (apples)   **Un ananas** (a pineapple)   **Les poires** (pears)   **Les bananes** (bananas)   **Un pamplemousse** (grapefruit)   **Les raisins** (grapes)

Les fraises (strawberries)   **Les abricots** (apricots)   **Les cerises** (cherries)   **Les oranges** (oranges)   **Les framboises** (raspberries)

Le potage (soup)

La salade (salad)

Les Viandes — **Meats (even Veggies need to know the right French)**

Le poulet (chicken)   **Les saucisses** (sausages)   **Le saucisson** (cooked sausage)   **Le biftec** (steak)   **Le porc** (pork)

Le boeuf (beef)   **Le jambon** (ham)   **L'agneau** (lamb)   **Le poisson** (fish)   **Les spaghettis à la bolognaise** (spaghetti bolognese)

Les Desserts — **Desserts**

Le Petit Déjeuner — **Breakfast**

Une crêpe (pancake)

au chocolat (with chocolate)

Un yaourt (yoghurt)

Les céréales (cereal)   **Le chocolat chaud** (hot chocolate)   **La confiture** (jam)

Du pain (bread)   **Le miel** (honey)

Les croissants (croissants)   **Le beurre** (butter)   **Un oeuf à la coque** (boiled egg)

Drink Vocabulary

To wash down your food there's nothing better than a refreshing drink — and this lovely vocab will really help you out with role-plays in restaurants or cafés. So get learning.

Un verre de... — A glass of... (but just the one)

la bière	*beer*
la limonade	*lemonade*
le jus d'orange	*orange juice*

le lait	*milk*
le vin rouge	*red wine*
le vin blanc	*white wine*

Une boîte de ... — A can of ...

le pop	*soda*
la bière blonde	*lager*

Une bouteille de... — A bottle of...

eg: *une bouteille d'eau minérale a bottle of mineral water*

1) '*Un citron pressé*' is freshly squeezed lemon juice. It's very popular in France.

2) '*Un diabolo*' is cordial and lemonade, and can be bought in many flavours:

Un diabolo

fraise	*strawberry*
citron	*lemon*
framboise	*raspberry*
cassis	*blackcurrant*
orange	*orange*
grenadine	*pomegranate*
pêche	*peach*
menthe	*mint*
pomme	*apple*

Try one sometime. They're delicious and refreshing!

Une tasse de... — A cup of...

le café	*coffee*
le café crème/au lait	*white coffee*
le thé	*tea*
le chocolat chaud	*hot chocolate*

Food and drink vocab — a recipe for Exam success...

Lots of lovely tasty _food words_ and some varied and refreshing hot and cold _drink words_ to wash them all down with. There's plenty of vocab here on these two pages — and you really need to _learn it_ before you go any further in this section. So stop a minute and make a big list of all the vocab. Then cover it up and practise writing it out over and over until it's sorted in your head.

Eating Out — Restaurants

Right — for the Exam you've got to be able to read the menu, order your meal and respond to whatever the waiter says. That means you've got to get this little lot learned thoroughly.

Ordering Food in a Restaurant is easy

1) The essential expressions for _HOW_ to _order politely_ are:
   a) Je voudrais + item + s'il vous plaît   _I would like ... please_
   b) Puis-je avoir + item + s'il vous plaît   _May I have ... please_

2) Now _WHAT_ to order. The first thing you need to ask the garçon
   or the serveuse (the waiter/ess) for is '_le Menu_'
   Puis-je avoir le menu s'il vous plaît? = May I have the menu please?

Le menu	_the menu_	Suggestion du chef	_the chef's suggestion_
La carte	_more expensive menu_	Le plat du patron	_recommended special_
Le plat du jour	_the meal of the day_	Le couvert	_the cover charge_
Les hors d'oeuvres	_the starters_	Un supplément de	_an extra charge of_
L'entrée	_the first course_	Boisson comprise	_drink included_
Le plat principal	_the main course_	Prix fixe	_fixed price_
La spécialité de la maison	_speciality of the restaurant_	Boisson non comprise	_drink not included_
La carte des vins	_the wine list_	Service compris	_service included_

3) Use the Menu below to help you _recognise_ the _waiter's remarks_:

Menu Détente

84 F

Prix net - Boisson comprise

Le Potage du Patron ou La Salade composée
ou L'Entrée du Jour
****
1 de nos Petits Plats sélectionnés par le Patron
ou
1 des Suggestions Campanile
****
Le BUFFET de fromages ou Le BUFFET de Desserts
ou Un Sorbet au choix

Waiter	_Bonjour monsieur!_	
You	Bonjour. Puis-je avoir le menu s'il vous plaît?	(May I have the menu please)
Waiter	_Voilà monsieur! Vous désirez monsieur?_	(Here you are sir. And what would you like sir?)
You	Pour commencer, je voudrais l'entrée du jour	(To start with I would like ....)
Waiter	_Et comme plat principal monsieur?_	(And what about the main course?)
You	Je prendrai "Une suggestion Campanile"	(I'll have one of the restaurant's suggestions)
Waiter	_Et comme dessert monsieur?_	(And what about the dessert?)
You	Un sorbet au citron s'il vous plaît	(A lemon sorbet please)
Waiter	_Et comme boisson monsieur?_	(And what about the drink sir?)
You	Du vin rouge s'il vous plaît	(Red wine please)
Waiter	_Ce sera tout monsieur?_	(Will that be all, sir?)
You	Oui merci	(Yes, thank you)

Role-plays like this are dead common in the Exam, so practise hard! It's best to be really polite — you'll pick up extra marks for it. So don't forget the basics:
Bonjour Monsieur, _S'il vous plaît_, _Merci Monsieur_, _Au revoir Monsieur_

The house special — a six bedroomed semi please...

Once again loads of vocab which you need to _learn_. Remember, you won't always have a posh restaurant in the role play — you may just have a café scene, so learn the _everyday stuff_, too.

Eating Out — Cafés

Time to get to grips with the menu now — you'll find there are lots of _technical names_ and _posh sounding words_ here, like in any restaurant. But don't worry, just keep _practising_ and you'll be fine.

Meats, Vegetables, Fish and Desserts

Les Viandes — the different types of Meat

Le poulet	chicken
Le boeuf	beef
Le porc	pork
Un steak	a steak
Des saucisses	sausages
Une côtelette de porc	a pork chop
Une omelette	an omelet

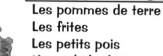

Les Légumes — Vegetables

Les pommes de terre	potatoes
Les frites	chips
Les petits pois	peas
Une salade de tomates	a tomato salad
Une salade de laitue	a lettuce salad
Des champignons	mushrooms
Des haricots verts	green beans

Les Poissons — Fish

Le poisson grillé	grilled fish
Les fruits de mer	Sea food
La truite au beurre	trout cooked in butter
Les crustacés	crabs, lobsters and scampi

You may want fish for the main course

So learn: "Moi, je prendrai du poisson"
As for me, I'll have the fish
"Je voudrais les crevettes"
I would like the prawns

Les Desserts — Desserts

Make sure you learn the most common dessert names:

une glace	an ice cream
une glace à la vanille	a vanilla ice cream
une glace à la fraise	a strawberry ice cream
une glace au chocolat	a chocolate ice cream
une tarte aux pommes	an apple pie
un gâteau	a cake
un gâteau au chocolat	a chocolate cake

REMEMBER: The waiter will ask you "_Et comme dessert Monsieur?_" If you learn all these and have a picture to respond to, you'll never go wrong in the Exam. Just don't forget to keep on practising.

> ### When you finish a meal ask the waiter for "L'addition" (the bill)

eg: Puis-je avoir l'addition s'il vous plaît?   _Can I have the bill please?_

Booking a Table over the Telephone

You may need to book a table (_réserver une table_) on the telephone for a number of people:

Patron	Allo, ici le Restaurant "Le Coq Noir"	_Hello, This is the Coq Noir Restaurant_
You	Je voudrais réserver une table svp	_I would like to book a table please_
Patron	C'est pour quand monsieur?	_When is it for sir?_
You	C'est pour mercredi le 10 août	_It's for Wednesday the 10th of August_
Patron	Et c'est pour combien de personnes?	_And it's for how many people?_
You	Pour quatre personnes, s'il vous plaît	_For four people please_
Patron	Et c'est pour quelle heure, monsieur?	_And for what time sir?_
You	C'est pour vingt heures	_It's for eight in the evening_
Patron	Bon, très bien monsieur! À mercredi!	_Fine sir! See you on Wednesday!_

A revolving restaurant — that's turning the tables...

You'll come across Restaurant topics in the Speaking, Listening and Reading Exams — you wouldn't book a table or order your meal in writing, after all. If you've learnt the names for food on P.54 and P.55 as well as the _extra vocabulary_ on this page, you won't go far wrong.

Recipes, Likes and Dislikes

Sometimes you can be given a recipe in the Reading or Listening papers — so learn this vocab now.

Les Recettes — Recipes (for disaster perhaps)

You'll need your Imperatives so look back over P.22. Some useful ones are — Préparez, Coupez, Mélangez, Ajoutez, Mettez, Faites Cuire, Râpez

Préparez les légumes   prepare the vegetables
Coupez les tomates   chop the tomatoes
Mélangez le lait et les oeufs   mix the milk and the eggs
Ajoutez le sel et l'ail   add the salt and the garlic
Mettez la viande dans *une casserole*   put the meat in a saucepan
                        ...*une poêle*   ...a frying pan
Faites cuire pour une heure   cook for an hour
Râpez le fromage   grate the cheese

Expressing Opinions About Food

Another good one for the Exam is talking about what food you *like* and *dislike*. It's always a top idea to say something about whether you *enjoyed* your meal if you're doing a *food role-play*:

1) Use:

J'aime + noun + plus que + noun

(I like .... more than ....)

J'aime la salade plus que les frites
I like salad more than chips

Non merci, je n'aime pas ça

(No thanks, I don't like that)

Non merci, je n'aime pas le poisson
No thanks, I don't like fish

2) Use:

C'est/c'était + délicieux/excellent

eg: C'est délicieux   *It is delicious*
        C'était excellent   *It was excellent*
        J'ai très bien mangé *I've eaten very well*

3) Use: **Item of food + était/étaient + adjective**

eg: La soupe était parfaite!
       The soup was perfect!

Les pommes de terre étaient merveilleuses!
The potatoes were marvellous!

The most important thing of all is to say *as much as you can* in your role-play — if you've learned all the vocab you may as well use it, and it'll get you *extra marks* if you show you can use it properly.

A winter recipe — cooking up a storm perhaps...

More food vocab I'm afraid — but this is really useful Exam material, so get it learned. Don't forget your *imperatives* for recipes, and practise *opinions on food*. They sound nicer in French...

Complaining, Enough and Too Much

Complaints are all very well — but you need to be able to tell the waiter if everything's alright too.

Making Complaints — Ça ne va pas!

It's dead important you make any complaint to a waiter politely — it gets you better marks and it means they're more likely to put a mistake right:

Use:

Ça ne va pas!	Il y a un problème!
(This isn't right!)	(There's a problem!)

eg: C'est froid!   Ce n'est pas cuit!
      (It's cold)   (It's not cooked!)

Let's talk portions — Enough, More, Too Much

Use:

J'ai assez mangé!
I've had enough!

Ça suffit!
That's enough!

Encore des frites, s'il vous plaît.
More chips please

Je prends un peu de vin
I'll have a little wine

C'est trop!
It's too much!

REMEMBER: after Encore use du/de la/de l'/des

To ask for things:

Donnez-moi	=	Give me
Je prends	=	I'll have

eg: Donnez-moi un peu de pain, s'il vous plaît   *Give me a bit of bread please*

      Je prends encore du café   *I'll have some more coffee*

All this food — I've had it up to here...

Phew — a nice easy page with plenty of pictures. Make sure you can tell a waiter about any _problems_ with your meal, and how to say you want _more_ or _less_ food. Most of all though, don't forget to be _polite_. Unless you're polite and use the _right forms_, you'll be chucking marks away.

Revision Summary for Section Five

Another section down — you'd better make room for some tip-top tasty revision questions.
Talk about boring — but they're something you just have to do I'm afraid. The most important
thing is to keep practising all the stuff you're learning. That way it stays fresh. So you've got
to start by answering as many of these questions as you can in French. Don't forget to give
plenty of detail. And don't bother looking back over the section before you have a go — that
won't help you in the Exams. You need to work out what you know and what you don't. Then
you can go back over the section and learn anything you're not sure about. And keep on doing
it — until you've got every answer on the page dead clear.

1) Give the names of five common vegetables and five common fruits.
2) Name two kinds of starter, three kinds of main course and two types of dessert.
3) Describe what you had for breakfast this morning.
4) How would you ask for: a) a glass of milk b) a lemonade c) a glass of red wine?
5) How would you ask for: a) a mint cordial b) a can of soda c) a bottle of mineral water
   d) a cup of white coffee e) a strawberry cordial?
6) How would you ask the waiter for a menu in a restaurant?
7) What is the French for: a) the dish of the day b) the chef's suggestion c) the cover charge
   d) service included e) the house speciality?
8) Jack is taking Rose out to dinner, but he's never been to a posh restaurant before. How
   would he order two starters of the day and two house specials for the main course? How
   would he ask for the wine menu? How would he order a bottle of the house red?
9) How would you order: a) grilled fish with chips and peas b) tomato salad c) pork chops
   with potatoes, mushrooms and beans?
10) How would you ask for: a) apple pie b) vanilla ice cream c) chocolate cake?
11) How would you ask for the bill at the end of the meal? How would you ask if there is a
    service charge?
12) How would you reserve a table for six over the phone, for 7.30 on Friday June 24th?
13) Leo is making dinner for Kate but he's not a very good cook. He's following a recipe he
    found in an old French cookbook. What does he have to do when it says: a) préparez les
    légumes b) mélangez le lait et les oeufs c) mettez les saucisses dans une poêle?
14) How would Kate say that Leo's cooking is delicious?
15) How would Kate say that she doesn't like sausages, eggs or vegetables?
16) Say whether you prefer chocolate or chips. Can you explain why?
17) How would you tell the waiter: a) you've had enough b) you want more potatoes c) you'd
    like a small glass of wine d) you would like some bread?
18) How would you tell the waiter your steak isn't cooked properly and your chips are cold?
19) How would you say that your meal was excellent?
20) Qu'est-ce que tu préfères manger? Tu aimes les légumes?
21) Qu'est-ce que tu aimes comme entrée? Tu aimes la viande?
22) Quel est ton dessert préféré?
23) Que manges-tu pour le petit déjeuner?
24) Quelle est ta boisson préférée?
25) Comment fait-on une omelette?
26) Tu aimes les frites plus que les pommes?
27) Name three kinds of food or drink that are popular in France, but that we don't really have in
    Britain.
28) Describe the menu for your ideal three-course meal in detail.

Accommodation — Hotels

This is always a *"favourite topic"* with the examiners, and it's quite useful if you're going on holiday to France as well. It's simple — just remember to *be polite*.

À l'hôtel — At the hotel (make sure you get a good Reception)

1) Start off by asking "Avez-vous une chambre libre?"   *Are there any rooms available?*

2) The receptionist might reply:

'Non, toutes les chambres sont complètes'   or   'Oui. Pour combien de personnes?'
No, all the rooms are taken   *Yes, for how many people?*

To say how many folk you want a room for:

Pour + number of people + personnes/adultes/enfants

(for .... people/adults/children)

eg: pour trois personnes   *for 3 people*
       pour deux adultes et un enfant   *for 2 adults and 1 child*

3) To say what sort of room you'd like:

"Je voudrais...............s'il vous plaît"

("I would like...............please")

une chambre pour une personne	*a single room*
deux personnes	*a double room*
une chambre de famille	*a family room*
une chambre avec un grand lit	*a room with a double bed*
une chambre avec douche	*a room with a shower*
avec salle de bains	*a room with a bath*

4) To say how long you'll be staying for:

du.........au   =   *from.......until*

du 14 juin *au* 18 juin   *from 14 June until 18 June*

pour une nuit/une semaine   *for 1 night/for 1 week*

JUIN						
1	2	3	4	5	6	7
8	9	10	11	12	13	14
15	16	17	18	19	20	21
22	23	24	25	26	27	28
29	30					

5) The all important thing to ask is the price (le prix):

C'est combien ....?

(How much is it...............?)

C'est combien par jour?	*How much is it per day?*
C'est combien par personne?	*How much is it per person?*
Je la prends	*I'll take it*
Non, je ne la prends pas, c'est trop cher.	*No, I won't take it, it's too expensive*
Est-ce que le petit déjeuner est compris?	*Is breakfast included?*

6) To book in advance: **Je voudrais réserver..............**

(I would like to reserve.........)

Je voudrais réserver une chambre pour deux personnes pour deux nuits.
I'd like to reserve a room for 2 people for 2 nights.

Hotels and Youth Hostels

At the hotel — À l'hôtel : Finding Your Way Around

1) The receptionist will tell you where to find your room:

au rez-de-chaussée	on the ground floor
au premier/deuxième étage	on the first/second floor
prenez l'ascenseur	take the lift
prenez l'escalier	take the stairs
voilà la clef	here's the key
avez-vous des bagages?	do you have any luggage?

You might also be asked to "remplir une fiche" (*fill in a form*)

2) Other things you might want to ask are:

Où sont les toilettes?!!

Où est/sont........?

(Where is/are.........?)

Où est le parking?　　Where's the car park?

Où sont les toilettes?　　Where are the toilets?

At the youth hostel — À l'auberge de jeunesse (f)

This is practically the same as booking into a hotel, with a few subtle *differences*.

1) Ask "*Avez-vous des places pour ce soir?*"　Do you have any beds for this evening?

2) You'll be asked "*Pour combien de personnes?*"　For how many people?

You need to answer:　**_Pour_ + _number_ + _personnes_**

In a youth hostel you'll need to say how many people there are of each sex:　Pour deux filles et trois garçons
For two girls and three boys

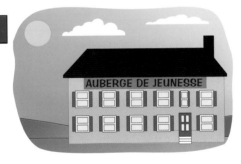

3) You may need to hire sheets if you've forgotten to bring them:　Est-ce que je peux louer des draps?
Can I hire some sheets?

Signs of the times

These are signs you'll need to recognise wherever you go:

PRIVÉ
Private

En PANNE
Out of Order

COMPLET
Full

CHAMBRES LIBRES
Rooms Available

ACCUEIL
Reception

CHAMBRES TOUT CONFORT
Comfortable rooms

Hotels are so polite — they're always accommodating...

Plenty of stuff to be *learnt* here, but it's all broken up into *chunks*. Work your way through it a *chunk at a time*, and you'll soon be able to arrange yourself comfortable and reasonably priced hotel accommodation anywhere in the French-speaking world...and get top marks in the Exam.

Camping

The French love "_la vie en plein air_" (the outdoor life) and camping is _very popular_, so even if it isn't your kind of thing you've got _to know_ how to _book into a campsite_.

At the Campsite — _Au Camping_

Booking into a campsite is basically the _same_ as booking into a hotel, except that some of the _vocabulary_ is different — and you'll be staying in a tent.

la tente
(tent)

la caravane
(caravan)

J'ai oublié l'ouvre - boîte

J'adore la vie en plein air!

le campeur
(camper)

l'emplacement
(pitch)

le sac de couchage
(sleeping bag)

le feu
(fire)

la lampe de poche
(torch)

1) To Book In:

Je voudrais un (des) emplacement(s) + pour + ...

(I would like a (some) pitch(es) for............)

eg: ....pour deux tentes
I want pitches for two tents
        ....pour une caravane
I want a pitch for a caravan
.........pour deux tentes pour deux nuits
I want pitches for two tents for two nights

2) To say How Many of You There Are:

Il y a + number + personnes/adultes/enfants

eg: Il y a deux adultes et trois enfants   _There are two adults and three children_

Imperfect tents — isn't that in the grammar section...

More booking in, and a little bit more _vocabulary_ for the campsite. Just think, if you were camping instead of revising, you could be having as much fun as the two people in the picture.

Camping Carry On

Once you're on site there are all sorts of things you need to know about — say rules and facilities.

At the Campsite - <u>Au Camping</u>: Facilities and Activities

1) You may want to ask what facilities there are at the campsite. Use:

Est-ce qu'il y a + facility + au camping

(Is there + facility + at the campsite?)

une piscine	*swimming pool*
des lavabos	*wash basins*
des poubelles	*dustbins*
un restaurant	*a restaurant*
un magasin	*shop*

un bac à linge	*sink for washing clothes*
un bac à vaisselle	*sink for washing dishes*
de l'eau potable	*drinking water*
un bar	*a bar*

2) Other phrases you might need to describe your camping holiday:

dresser une tente	*to pitch a tent*
se bronzer	*to sunbathe*
se baigner	*to swim*
barboter	*to paddle*
le camping est près de la mer	*the campsite is near the sea*
le camping est près d'un lac	*the campsite is near to a lake*

Sticking to the Rules — <u>Les Règles</u>

Wherever you go, there'll be <u>rules</u> you have to follow (according to the examiners anyway). So, just in case you need to know what you're <u>not allowed to do</u>, learn the phrases below:

Défense de....	=	*it is forbidden to...*
Interdit de....	=	*it is forbidden to...*
Ne....pas	=	*don't...*
Prière de.....	=	*please...*

DÉFENSE DE FUMER

Staying at Someone's House — <u>Rester à la maison de quelqu'un</u>

Another favourite <u>*Exam topic*</u> is going to stay with friends in France, or having French visitors in your own home. There's a lot you need to be <u>*able to say*</u>, or <u>*understand*</u> when it's said to you (see also P.38):

Comment vous-appelez vous?

Parlez-vous français?

Je peux te tutoyer?

Comment allez-vous?

D'où êtes-vous?

Quel âge avez-vous?

Accommodation's a big topic — you need staying power..

It's not just tents, you know. It's a whole wide world of fun and adventure. The section in the middle is <u>*important*</u> — signs saying what's forbidden are the sort of things that sneak their way into the Reading Exam. <u>*Cover*</u> and <u>*scribble*</u> and get it fixed in your brain — and <u>*keep it there*</u>.

Tourist Information

If you want any *holiday information* you'll have to use *'l'office de tourisme'* (the tourist information office) — get the vocab learned:

Les Renseignements — Information

1) There are two ways of saying tourist information office:

l'office de tourisme (m)
le syndicat d'initiative

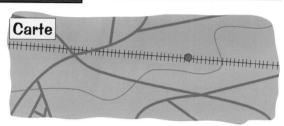

2) Practise asking for a few different things using this phrase.

To ask: **Avez-vous + item + s'il vous plaît?**

(have you got............please?)

un plan de la ville	*a map of the town*
une carte	*a map*
une liste d'hôtels	*a list of hotels*
une liste de campings	*a list of campsites*
une liste de restaurants	*a list of restaurants*

un dépliant sur...	*a leaflet about...*
une brochure sur...	*a brochure about...*
une brochure touristique	*a tourist brochure*
un guide de...	*a guide to ...*
un horaire des trains	*a train timetable*

3) You can also ask about what there is to do in the town:

Qu'est-ce qu'il y a à faire ici? (What is there to do here?)

Hopefully there's plenty going on:

Il y a...	**There is/there are...**
des spectacles	*shows*
un cinéma	*a cinema*
un théâtre	*a theatre*
des musées (m)	*museums*
un zoo	*a zoo*
une fête foraine	*a fun fair*
une patinoire	*an ice rink*

un centre de loisirs	*a leisure centre*
une cathédrale	*a cathedral*
le cimetière	*the cemetery*
le marché	*the market*
la statue	*the statue*
des monuments	*the monuments*
le parc	*the park*
un club	*a club*
une plage	*a beach*
un lac	*a lake*
une rivière	*a river*

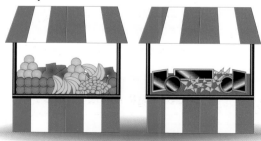

An information office — could be a tourist trap...

Another page simply bursting at the seams with juicy vocabulary about the tourist information office — it's dead important for role-plays and for real life too maybe. *Cover* it, *write* it, *learn* it.

Seeing the Sights

At the tourist office you'll need to ask the right questions — and maybe get directions where to go.

Asking at *le Syndicat d'Initiative*

1) *They might tell you:*

On peut.........

(You can ......)

faire du ski nautique	*go water skiing*
faire un tour en bateau	*go for a boat trip*
partir en excursion	*go on a trip*
faire des promenades	*go for walks*
faire des randonnées à cheval	*go pony trekking*

se bronzer	*sunbathe*
nager	*swim*
faire du vélo	*go cycling*
faire des courses	*go shopping*

You can ask for more information about any of these attractions:

Je voudrais des renseignements sur........... s'il vous plaît.

(I would like some information about.........please)

2) *You may need to ask for directions to any of the places mentioned.*

Pour aller à la banque s'il vous plaît?

Pour aller à + place + s'il vous plaît?

(How do I get to + place + please?)

Est-ce que + place + est loin d'ici?

(Is it far to + place?)

For direction words see next page

Other places you might need to ask for directions to are:

la banque	*the bank*
la poste	*the post office*
le centre-ville	*the town centre*
la gare	*the railway station*
la gare routière	*the bus station*
le médecin	*the doctor*
l'hôpital (m)	*the hospital*

Est-ce que la pharmacie est loin d'ici?

3) *You can also buy tickets and reserve seats and accommodation at the 'syndicat d'initiative'.*

Je voudrais un billet pour.........	*I'd like a ticket for........*
Je voudrais réserver des billets pour	*I'd like to reserve some tickets for*
le spectacle son et lumière.	*the 'son et lumière' show*
Je voudrais réserver une chambre dans un hôtel.	*I'd like to reserve a room in a hotel*

And the all important question (for your wallet anyway):

C'est combien?   **How much is it?**

Join the tourist board — give directions to your life...

More things to ask about at the *tourist information office*. Just think, you could ask for information on almost anything (within reason), and they'd have to do their best to find out. You really do need to learn this vocab if you want to understand what's going on in a *role-play*. So learn it right now.

Giving Directions

These are a tremendous mark-winner in the Exam — they turn up in role-plays and often in the Listening paper as well. Start by learning the key phrases *pour aller au/à la/à l'/aux* and *où est.*

Asking the Way — Get lost mate

1) Always start with "Excusez-moi madame/monsieur" (Excuse me Sir/Madam) followed by:

où est + location + s'il vous plaît?

(Where is .... please?)

Pour aller + au/à la/à l'/aux + location + s'il vous plaît?

(How do I get to .... please?)

eg: Où est la poste s'il vous plaît?
Where is the post office please?

Pour aller au syndicat d'initiative, s'il vous plaît?
Where is the tourist information office please?

2) If you want to know whether the town has a certain facility, use:

Est-ce qu'il y a + place + ici + s'il vous plaît?

(Is there a .... here, please?)

eg: Est-ce qu'il y a une poste ici, s'il vous plaît?
Is there a post office here?

Est-ce qu'il y a une piscine dans la ville?
Is there a swimming pool in the town?

This is top stuff for all the Exam papers, so get it learned.

I get around — Directions

1) The two most important phrases to remember are:

à gauche	à droite
to/on the left	*to/on the right*

2) Use one of the following three verbs to give your instructions:

PRENDRE = *to take*
TOURNER = *to turn*
ALLER = *to go*

Prenez la première rue à droite
Take the first street on the right

Prenez la deuxième rue à gauche
Take the second street on the left

Tournez à gauche
Turn left

Tournez à droite
Turn right

Allez tout droit
Go straight on

Finding Your Way Around

You could be given a simple _map_ in the _Exam_, and have to tell someone how to get from one place to another, or to follow some _instructions_ and see where you end up. Make sure you learn all this.

Some Spectacular Phrases for More Detailed _Directions_

en face de	opposite	à côté de	next to
près de	near to	loin de	far from
à ... kilomètres de	....kilometres from	là-bas	over there
au bout de	at the end of	après	after
derrière	behind	devant	in front of
au coin	on the corner	prochain	next
sur la gauche	on the left	sur la droite	on the right
puis	then	continuer	to continue

Est-ce que je dois prendre l'autobus? — _Do I need to take the bus?_
Je suis perdu — _I'm lost_
Est-ce que la gare est près d'ici? — _Is the station near here?_

Always remember to say _"merci"_

The map shows various places that you might need to ask directions to. Practise saying how you could get to each one from, say, the church, and then from the café...

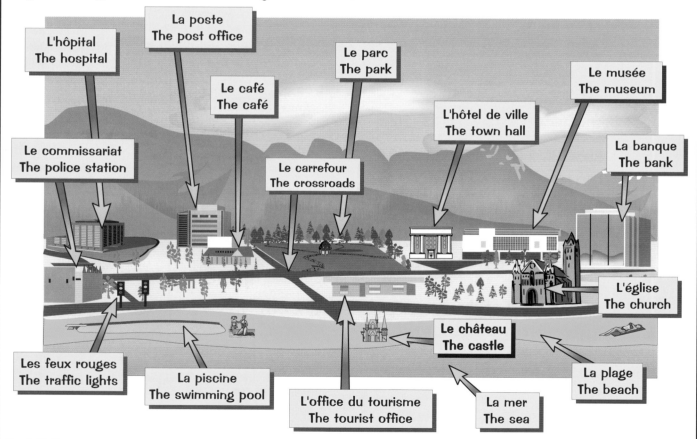

L'hôpital — The hospital
La poste — The post office
Le café — The café
Le parc — The park
Le musée — The museum
L'hôtel de ville — The town hall
La banque — The bank
Le commissariat — The police station
Le carrefour — The crossroads
L'église — The church
Les feux rouges — The traffic lights
La piscine — The swimming pool
L'office du tourisme — The tourist office
Le château — The castle
La mer — The sea
La plage — The beach

Don't panic — I've got this all mapped out...

There's a lot of vocabulary on this page and the one before, and, yes, you have to learn all of it. Remember, you need to be able to _understand_ directions that are given to you, as well as give them yourself, otherwise there's _no point_ in asking in the first place — this means that you need to know the _names_ of all sorts of places in town. So time to get it memorised — no brain no gain.

Bank And Post Office

You're going to need to *change some money* at some point during your trip to France. It's just as easy as doing it in England — except you have to do it *in French* of course.

À la Banque — At the Bank

1) To change your money you need to go to *'le bureau de change'* (the exchange office). You should also check out *'le cours du change'* (the exchange rate).

2) You'll need to say:

> **Je voudrais changer + money + en francs**

(I would like to change + money + into francs)

> **Je voudrais encaisser un chèque / un chèque de voyage**

(I would like to cash a cheque / a travellers' cheque)

Je voudrais encaisser un chèque de voyage

Banque

3) You need to say how much money you want to change.

Je voudrais changer...	*I want to change...*
une livre/vingt livres sterling	*one pound/twenty pounds*

And that's it. You might have to pay *'une commission'* (a commission), and show *'une pièce d'identité'* (identification).

4) Other words to do with banks that you need to know are:

économiser	*to save*	une carte bancaire	*a bank card*
faire des économies	*to save money*	une carte de crédit	*a credit card*
emprunter	*to borrow*	un portefeuille	*a wallet*
prêter	*to lend*	un porte-monnaie	*a purse*
signer	*to sign*	un sac à main	*a handbag*
retirer de l'argent	*to take money out*	un carnet de chèques	*a cheque book*
une pièce	*a coin*	la monnaie	*change*
un billet	*a note*	l'argent de poche	*pocket money*

À la Poste — At the Post Office

You'll need the post office for sending all those postcards to your friends back home.

1) Here are the essential bits of vocab:

une lettre	*a letter*	un colis	*a parcel/packet*
une carte postale	*a postcard*	le courrier	*the mail*
un mandat-poste	*a postal order*	fragile	*fragile*
par avion	*by air*	urgent	*urgent*
une lettre par avion	*airmail letter*	l'adresse (f)	*address*
une lettre recommandeé	*a registered letter*	une boîte aux lettres	*a post box*
un télégramme	*a telegram*	les heures de levée(f.pl)	*collection times*
un timbre	*a stamp*	le facteur	*the postman*
un timbre d'un franc	*a one-franc stamp*	le guichet	*the counter*

2) In the post office: **Je voudrais........s'il vous plaît?**

envoyer une lettre/une carte postale	un timbre pour une lettre pour l'Angleterre	mettre à la poste
to send a letter/a postcard	*a stamp for a letter to England*	*to post*

I went to the Left Bank in Paris — but there's no cash...

Lovely-jubbly — some smashing bank and post office vocab. These topics could come up anywhere, not just on holiday, so make sure you've got the vocab and phrases sorted. Get going.

Revision Summary for Section Six

Time for some more of those amazingly wonderful revision questions — they've got to be done I'm afraid. Holidays are a big favourite in the Exams — and as long as you know your vocab you can pick up plenty of easy marks here. Remember — the key is to learn the basic phrases and then adapt them to any situation you get given in the Exams. So start by working through these questions to see what you know. It doesn't matter if you can't get all of them first time. Go back over the section and then work through the questions again. By the time you're finished practising them you should be able to give the answers in your sleep. So get on with it.

1) How would you ask for a hotel room for two people with a shower for one week?
2) How would you ask what the price of a room is: a) per person b) per day?
3) How would you ask if breakfast is included?
4) What would you say on the phone to reserve a hotel room for two people for two nights next weekend?
5) You are scared of heights. How would you ask if you can have a room on the ground floor?
6) Travelling around France you arrive in a Youth Hostel one night. How would you ask if there are any beds for the evening? Tell them you need beds for three girls and three boys. How would you ask if you can hire some sheets?
7) What do the following signs mean: a) accueil b) complet c) en panne?
8) What is the French for outdoor life? What is the French for: a) tin opener b) sleeping bag c) torch d) tent?
9) How would you ask for a pitch for four tents for one night? Tell the owner there are four boys and two girls in your group.
10) How would you ask if there is: a) a swimming pool b) a shop c) drinking water d) a bar?
11) How would you say that you want to: a) sunbathe b) pitch a tent c) go swimming?
12) What does 'interdit de nager' mean?
13) Write a paragraph describing a camping trip using at least five key phrases from this section.
14) How would you ask at the Tourist Office if they have: a) a list of campsites b) a map of the town c) a leaflet about the sights of the city d) a train timetable?
15) How would you ask if the town has: a) a zoo b) a theatre c) a cemetery?
16) Kate has gone on holiday to France. On her first day she goes to the Tourist Office where she meets Jean-Claude. How does Kate ask Jean-Claude for information about: a) swimming b) pony-trekking c) sunbathing d) shopping?
17) How would Kate ask Jean-Claude for directions to the town centre? How would she ask if the Post Office was far from here?
18) How would Jean-Claude ask the Tourist Office manager for two tickets to the son et lumière show for this evening?
19) How would Kate ask the way to the park for the son et lumière show?
20) Give detailed directions from your school to the main shopping centre near you.
21) Look at the map on page 68. Give directions to someone wanting to go: a) from the traffic lights to the park b) from the museum to the church c) from the town hall to the swimming pool d) from the castle to the police station.
22) How would you ask to change a travellers' cheque at the bank? Ask what the exchange rate is. Ask if you can change pounds sterling to francs.
23) Kate is in the Post Office trying to send a letter to Leo. How would she ask for three stamps to England?
24) You've got to go back to the bank because you forgot your wallet. You ask for directions. A helpful man says: "Pour aller à la banque prenez la troisième rue à droite, allez tout droit jusqu'aux feux rouges, tournez à gauche et la banque est à droite." Where should you go?

Jobs and Employment

It's dead important you can talk about your future in the _Speaking_ and the _Writing_ Exams — so spend some time learning this vocab for jobs.

Les Emplois — On the Job

un agent immobilier	an estate agent
un agent de police	a policeman
un/une bibliothécaire	a librarian
un chef de cuisine	a chef
un/une chirurgien(ne)	a surgeon
un/une coiffeur(euse)	a hairdresser
un comptable	an accountant

un boucher	a butcher
un chauffeur	a chauffeur
un acteur	an actor
une actrice	an actress
un arpenteur	a surveyor
un avocat	a lawyer
un banquier	a banker

un danseur	a male dancer
une danseuse	a female dancer
un dentiste	a dentist
un électricien	an electrician
un étudiant	a student
une étudiante	a female student
un facteur	a postman
un homme d'affaires	a businessman
une hôtesse de l'air	an air-hostess

une infirmière	a nurse
un ingénieur	an engineer
un mécanicien	a mechanic
un médecin	a doctor
un musicien	a musician
un pharmacien	a chemist
un plombier	a plumber
un pompier	a fireman
un professeur	a teacher

une puéricultrice	a nursery nurse
une réceptionniste	a receptionist
une secrétaire	a secretary
un vendeur	a salesman
une vendeuse	a saleswoman
une maquilleuse	a make-up artist

Talking about work — Parler Au Sujet De Travail

You've got to be able to talk about the kind of work people do — and where they do it:

Je travaille dans une agence	I work in an agency
Il travaille dans une banque	He works in a bank
Elle travaille dans un bureau	She works in an office
Nous travaillons dans une usine	We work in a factory

Employment — it's too much like hard work...

Obviously you need to be able to say what jobs your parents and relatives do and what jobs you'd like to do when you leave school. But don't forget, lots of these words could come up in the Reading, Listening and Writing papers, too — so you need to _learn_ them _all_ very carefully.

Future Plans

You'll probably be asked what you want to do after you leave school at some point in the *Exam*.

Ton Choix — *Your Choice in the World of Work*

When you are being asked about what you intend to do when you leave school, the question will be as follows:

Que + feras-tu + lorsque + tu quitteras + l'école?

(What will you do when you leave school?)

If you know which particular job you intend to do (or don't want to do), your answer will be:

Je veux + être + job

(I want + to be + job)

Je ne veux pas + être + job

(I don't want to be + job)

Je veux être chirurgien

One big difference between French and English is that you *don't* need the '*un*' or '*une*' before the name of the job in French, whereas you do need the 'a' or 'an' in English.

Other Examples:

Je veux être comptable	*I want to be an accountant*
Je ne veux pas être facteur	*I don't want to be a postman*
Il veut être dentiste	*He wants to be a dentist*
Elle ne veut pas être secrétaire	*She doesn't want to be a secretary*

Les Études Avancées — *Further Studies*

If you've made up your mind to go to *University* after you leave school, you'll need to say which *subject* you intend to study. Here's how to do that:

J'espère + aller + à + l'université. J'y + étudierai + SUBJECT

(I hope to go to University. I shall study + SUBJECT)

Matières — *Subjects*

le dessin	*art*			
le droit	*law*			
le tourisme	*tourism*			
la biologie	*biology*			
la chimie	*chemistry*			
la géographie	*geography*	la musique	*music*	
l'histoire (f)	*history*	la physique	*physics*	
l'informatique (f)	*I.C.T*	la psychologie	*psychology*	
les langues vivantes	*modern languages*	les sciences économiques	*economics*	
la littérature	*literature*	les sciences politiques	*politics*	
les maths	*maths*	la sociologie	*sociology*	

They say the future's a lottery — perhaps I'm a winner...

Once you've got jobs sorted you need to be able to answer questions about what you want to do in the future. Remember the *form* of the question (with the future tense) and how to *answer*. Don't forget how to say that you hope to go to university — if that's what you want.

Shopping

It's fun to go shopping, especially in a foreign country. Here are the names of some _French shops_ and the items you're likely to find in them. So don't go looking for books in a boucherie.

Magasin	Articles	Shop	Shopping items
une boucherie	agneau (m), boeuf (m), porc (m)	butcher's	lamb, beef, pork
une boulangerie	pain (m), petits pains (m pl)	baker's	bread, rolls
une confiserie	bonbons (m pl), chocolat (m)	confectioner's	sweets, chocolate
une épicerie	beurre (m), oeufs (m pl), sucre (m)	grocer's	butter, eggs, sugar
une fruiterie	bananes (f pl), oranges (f pl), pommes (f pl)	greengrocer's	bananas, oranges, apples
une librairie	livres (m pl), magazines (m pl)	bookshop	books, magazines
une papeterie	crayons (m pl), stylos (m pl), papier (m)	stationer's	pencils, pens, paper
une parfumerie	parfum (m)	perfumery	perfume
une pharmacie	comprimés (m pl), médicaments (m pl)	pharmacy	tablets, medecine
une poissonerie	huîtres (f pl), moules (f pl), poisson (m)	fishmonger's	oysters, mussels, fish
un supermarché	tout	supermarket	everything

Asking For Things you want to Buy

REMEMBER the two ways of asking for items which you have already learnt — they can be used again when you go shopping.

Je voudrais + un/une/des + item + s'il vous plaît
(I'd like + a/some + item + please)

Je peux avoir + un/une/des + item + s'il vous plaît
(May I have + a/some + article + please?)

Quantities, Weights and Measures

Make sure you know your numbers (see P.26) — then quantities should be pretty easy:

Je peux avoir six œufs, s'il vous plaît?	_May I have 6 eggs, please?_
Je voudrais deux oranges, s'il vous plaît.	_I'd like 2 oranges, please._
Je peux avoir cinq stylos, s'il vous plaît?	_May I have 5 pens, please?_
Je voudrais une douzaine de pommes, s'il vous plaît.	_I'd like a dozen apples, please._

Like most countries in Europe the metric system is used for weights and measures. Study these examples.

Cent grammes de fromage (m)	_100g of cheese_
Cinq cents grammes de fraises (f pl)	_500g of strawberries_
Un kilo de pommes de terre (f pl)	_1kg of potatoes_
Deux kilos de pêches (f pl)	_2kg of peaches_
Un demi-litre de bière	_Half a litre of beer_
Un litre d'eau minérale	_A litre of mineral water_
Deux litres de vin rouge	_Two litres of red wine_

The purchasing experience — let's talk shop...

This page tells you the names of the shops where you'd buy various things. Remember the _two_ ways of asking for what you want. Don't forget, the weights and measures are all metric.

Buying Clothes

Shopping vocab can pop up in strange places in the Exam. In the _written paper_ you might have to write a statement about seeing a _thief_ and have to describe what they were _wearing_.

Clothes — Les Vêtements

Vêtements Hommes:

une cravate	_a tie_
un pantalon	_a pair of trousers_

Autres Vêtements:

des chaussettes	_socks_
une chemise	_a shirt_
un complet	_a suit_
un manteau	_a coat_
un pull (un pull-over)	_a pullover_
des chaussures	_shoes_
des sous-vêtements	_underclothes_

Vêtements Femmes:

une blouse	_a blouse_
une jupe	_a skirt_
une robe	_a dress_
un collant	_tights_

Les Couleurs — Colours

Remember that if colours are used as adjectives, they must agree with the noun they describe.

Look at these examples:

J'aime le bleu
I like blue

Ma chemise est bleue
My shirt is blue

Un pantalon vert
Green trousers

Colour	M sglr	Fem sglr	M plural	Fem plural
white	blanc	blanche	blancs	blanches
blue	bleu	bleue	bleus	bleues
brown	brun	brune	bruns	brunes
grey	gris	grise	gris	grises
yellow	jaune	jaune	jaunes	jaunes
black	noir	noire	noirs	noires
pink	rose	rose	roses	roses
red	rouge	rouge	rouges	rouges
green	vert	verte	verts	vertes

Taille — Size

This is the general word for _'size'_ although the word _'pointure'_ (f) is also used for hats (les chapeaux _(m pl)_) and shoes. The main words to watch out for are _grand/grande_ (large), _moyen/moyenne_ (medium) and _petit/petite_ (small). In clothes shops you may be asked the question _"Quelle est votre taille?"_ or _"Quelle est votre pointure?"_ (What size do you take?).

Le Salon d'Essayage — The Fitting Room

If you want to try an item of clothing on, it is only polite to ask if you may. The formula is:

Je peux essayer + ce/cet/cette/ces + item + s'il vous plaît?

(May I try on + this + item + please?)

Example:
Je peux essayer ce pantalon s'il vous plaît?
May I try on these trousers please?

> Remember the different forms of ce/cet/cette/ces for saying this and these. If you've forgotten, look back at P.3 in the Grammar Section.

Clothes shopping in the Exam — dressed for success...

Even if you have no intention of going clothes shopping in France, you need to know this stuff, because you can bet there'll be something about _clothes_ and _colours_ in the exam.

Discounts and Refunds

Here's some more ace vocab you'll need to help you shop till you drop — sounds painful really.

Les Grands Magasins — Department Stores

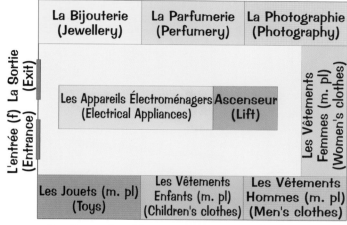

La Bijouterie (Jewellery)	La Parfumerie (Perfumery)	La Photographie (Photography)

L'entrée (f) (Entrance) / La Sortie (Exit)

Les Appareils Électroménagers (Electrical Appliances) | Ascenseur (Lift) | Les Vêtements Femmes (m. pl) (Women's clothes)

| Les Jouets (m. pl) (Toys) | Les Vêtements Enfants (m. pl) (Children's clothes) | Les Vêtements Hommes (m. pl) (Men's clothes) |

Le Rez-de-Chaussée (Ground Floor)

Le Restaurant (Restaurant)	La Musique (Music)	Le Ménage (Household Items)

L'Alimentation (Food)

Les Toilettes (f. pl) (Toilets) | Ascenseur (Lift) | Les Ordinateurs (m. pl) (Computers)

| L'Alimentation (Food) | L'Outillage (m) (Tools) | Les Téléviseurs (Televisions) |

Le Premier Étage (First Floor)

Les Soldes — Sales (Bargain Hunter alert)

If you go to these you may well pick up a bargain! Look out for other signs on shop windows, such as:

PRIX RÉDUIT!!

Reduced Price

RABAIS

Discount Prices

LIQUIDATION TOTALE!!

Everything at a greatly reduced price

TOUT DOIT DISPARAÎTRE!!

Everything must go!

Les Rabais — Discounts

If you want to know whether there's a discount on a group of items, use the following formula to ask:

Est-ce que vous vendez + ces + articles + au rabais?

(Do you sell + these + articles + at a discount?)

Examples:

Est-ce que vous vendez ces vins _au rabais_?   _Do you sell these wines at a discount?_

Est-ce que vous vendez ces outils _au rabais_?   _Do you sell these tools at a discount?_

Les Remboursements — Refunds

If you're not satisfied with something which you've bought and still have your till receipt, you may claim a refund. The phrase to use is:

Je voudrais + un remboursement + s'il vous plaît

(I'd like + a refund + please)

Learn this stuff now — you won't get your money back...

Some useful stuff to help you find your way around a department store — you wouldn't want to spend days stuck in a shop, unable to find your way out... Don't forget to _learn_ all these _new expressions_ — it's pretty likely that the discount signs will come up in the Reading Exam, and you might have to ask for a refund in the Speaking Exam. Just make sure you keep practising.

The Body

Parts of the Body — *Les Parties du Corps*

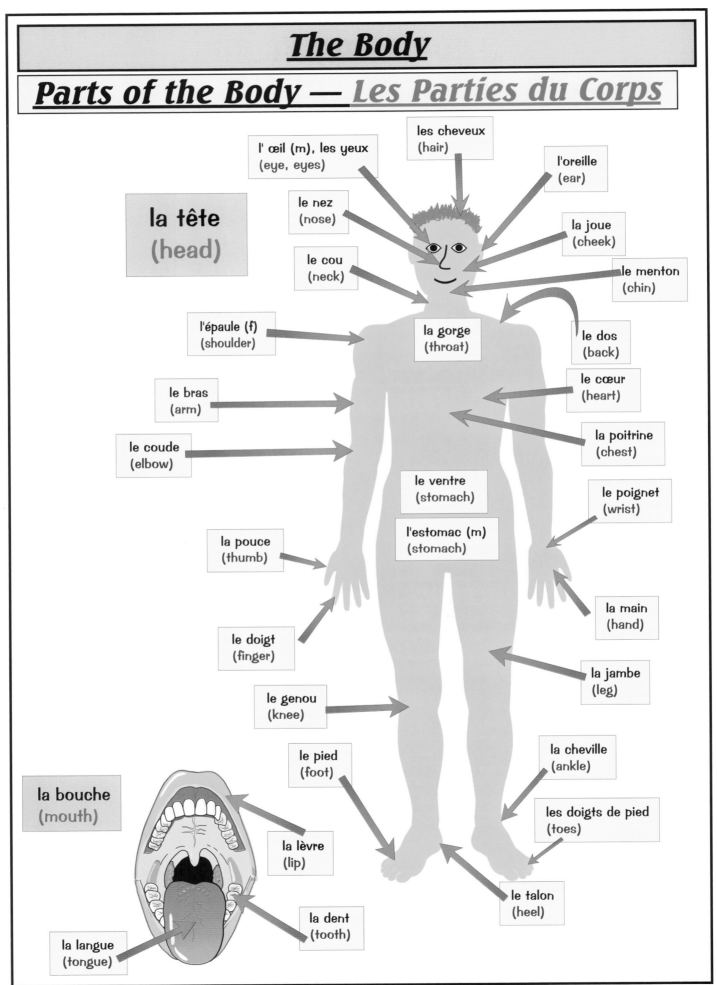

les cheveux (hair)

l' œil (m), les yeux (eye, eyes)

l'oreille (ear)

le nez (nose)

la joue (cheek)

la tête (head)

le cou (neck)

le menton (chin)

l'épaule (f) (shoulder)

la gorge (throat)

le dos (back)

le cœur (heart)

le bras (arm)

le coude (elbow)

la poitrine (chest)

le ventre (stomach)

le poignet (wrist)

l'estomac (m) (stomach)

la pouce (thumb)

le doigt (finger)

la main (hand)

la jambe (leg)

le genou (knee)

le pied (foot)

la cheville (ankle)

la bouche (mouth)

les doigts de pied (toes)

la lèvre (lip)

la dent (tooth)

le talon (heel)

la langue (tongue)

Going to the Doctor's

Illness is another Exam favourite. Examiners like to see you suffer, so get all this vocab sorted for illnesses and medicines — that'll cure them.

Saying Exactly What's Wrong with you

1) Use 'avoir mal à' + le/la/l'/les + the part of the body that hurts.

2) REMEMBER that when you use the preposition 'à' with le/la/l' /les, it becomes either au, à la, à l' or aux
(if you've forgotten this, look back at P.5)

3) So this is easy. All you need to do is use the right bit of 'avoir' and remember to change the 'à' bit.

eg: J'ai mal ...

... au ventre	I've got stomach ache
... à la tête	I've got a headache
... aux dents	I've got toothache
... à la gorge	I've got a sore throat

Here are some other phrases that might be useful if you don't feel well.

Je suis malade	I'm ill	se blesser	to hurt yourself
Je me sens bien	I feel well	se casser le bras	to break your arm
J' ai froid	I'm cold	saigner du nez	to have a nose bleed
J' ai chaud	I'm hot	avoir le mal de mer	to be seasick
Je suis enrhumé	I've got a cold	la fièvre	fever/temperature
J'ai la grippe	I've got flu	la douleur	pain
vomir	to be sick - literally!	tousser	to cough

Les Remèdes — Things can only Get Better

Of course, if you feel really ill you need to go to the <u>doctor</u>, or to the <u>chemist</u>, so here are some useful phrases;

Aller .... au médecin	to go to the doctor
.... au dentiste	to go to the dentist
.... à l'hôpital	to go to the hospital
.... à la pharmacie	to go to the chemist's

Prendre rendez-vous	to make an appointment
une ordonnance	a prescription

Je voudrais .... un sparadrap	I want a plaster
.... une bande	a bandage
.... un cachet d'aspirine	some aspirin
.... des comprimés	tablets

Surgery — how to get ahead in the medical world...

You'll need to remember the verb <u>avoir</u> for this bit. You've really got to know <u>how</u> to say that such and such a bit of you hurts, so it's time for the old '<u>cover</u>, <u>try it</u> and see how much you <u>remember</u>' trick. Same with the vocabulary in the orange and blue boxes. Try it at home...

Health

Right — here's some more medical vocab for your _Doctor's advice_ and for _prescriptions_.

Autres Problèmes de la Santé — **Other Health Problems**

une ampoule	a blister	une enflure	a swelling
l'appendicite (f)	appendicitis	une fracture	a fracture
une contusion	a bruise	l'insolation (f)	sunstroke
une coupure	a cut	mordre	to bite
se couper	to cut oneself	une morsure	a bite
la crampe	cramp	piquer	to sting
la diarrhée	diarrhoea	une piqûre	a sting

Les Conseils du Médecin — **The Doctor's Advice**

You need to understand what advice the Doc gives you — so make sure you've learned all of this lot:

Prenez ce médicament trois fois par jour
Take this medicine 3 times a day

médicament

Prenez ces comprimés deux fois par jour
Take these tablets twice a day

comprimés

Quand? — **When?**

après les repas	=	after meals
avant de manger	=	before eating
avant de se coucher	=	before going to bed
pendant les repas	=	during meals

Prenez ce sirop une fois par jour
Take this syrup once a day

sirop

Instructions Compliquées — **Complicated Instructions**

Don't worry, when you pick up your _ordonnance_ (f) (prescription) from the _pharmacien_ (m) (chemist), you should get instructions with whatever you have been prescribed, eg:

Dosage (m):	un comprimé	trois fois par jour	après les repas.
Dose:	_one tablet_	_three times a day_	_after meals_
Médicaments:	deux cuillerées à soupe	deux fois par jour	avant de manger.
Medicines:	_two tablespoonfuls_	_twice a day_	_before meals_
Enfants:	une cuillerée à soupe	une fois par jour	avec les repas.
Children:	_one tablespoonful_	_once a day_	_with meals_

Chemists — give them a taste of their own medicine...

Loads more top health related vocabulary on this page, and guess what — it needs _learning_. By you. It's important to know when to take medicine so learn the expressions for _x times a day_ and _before_ or _after meals_. All good stuff that'll be useful on holiday as well as in the Exams.

Lost and Found

Some folk just can't help losing things — but you _can't afford_ to lose any marks in the Exam. _Lost property_ is another topic examiners like — so don't forget to learn it.

Qu'est-ce que vous avez perdu? — What have you lost?

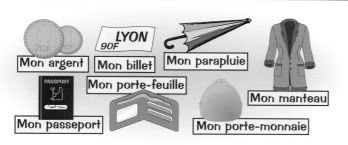

mon argent	my money
mon billet	my ticket
mon manteau	my coat
mon parapluie	umbrella
mon passeport	my passport
mon portefeuille	my wallet
mon porte-monnaie	my purse

mon sac	my bag
mon sac à dos	my rucksack
mon sac à main	my handbag
mon vélo	my bicycle
ma bague	ring
ma clé (or ma clef)	my key
ma montre	my watch

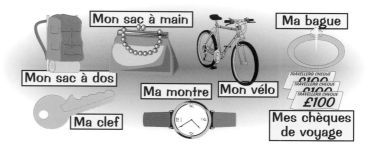

J'ai perdu + mon/ma/mes + item
(I've lost + my + item)

eg: J'ai perdu _mon_ billet   I've lost my ticket
J'ai perdu _ma_ clef   I've lost my key

1) You may need to _describe_ the item you've lost — remember your colours on P.74.
2) If you want to say _somebody else_ has lost something:

   eg: Il/Elle a perdu + _son_ passeport/_ses_ clefs/_sa_ montre
      He/She has lost his/her passport/his/her keys/his/her watch

> Look back to P.4 if you've forgotten how to use _possessive adjectives_

Au Bureau Des Objets Trouvés — At the Lost Property Office

Yep, the examiners love this setting for a role-play — either if you've lost something or if you've found it and are handing it in.

Use: **J'ai trouvé + item**

J'ai trouvé un parapluie	I've found an umbrella
J'ai trouvé une bague	I've found a ring
J'ai trouvé de l'argent	I've found some money
Mon père a trouvé un sac	My father has found a bag

Bureau des Objets Trouvés

NOM	Smith
PRÉNOM	John
ADDRESSE	12 North Street, Édimbourg, ÉCOSSE
NUMÉRO DE TÉLÉPHONE	0131-748-9992
OBJET TROUVÉ	Sac à main brun.

You may be given a '_formulaire_' (form) to be filled in, giving your name, address, telephone number and a description of the item which you've found. If you're really lucky you may receive a '_récompense_' (reward) if the object is claimed by its owner, or, more likely, a letter to thank you for the trouble you have taken.

All this vocab — don't lose your cool...

Keep your personal belongings close at hand, and you won't have to use this stuff in real life. The Exams, though, are quite a different matter. You've got to know the _vocabulary_ for the thing you've _lost or found_ — and you need to remember how to say it was yours, his or hers.

Train Travel

Travelling by train in France is a _pleasant experience_. The French have some of the _best trains_ in the world.

À la Gare — At the Station

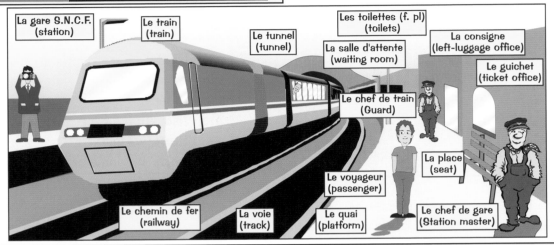

La gare S.N.C.F. (station)
Le train (train)
Le tunnel (tunnel)
Les toilettes (f. pl) (toilets)
La salle d'attente (waiting room)
La consigne (left-luggage office)
Le guichet (ticket office)
Le chef de train (Guard)
La place (seat)
Le voyageur (passenger)
Le chef de gare (Station master)
Le chemin de fer (railway)
La voie (track)
Le quai (platform)

Comment demander un billet — How to ask for a ticket

You should know where you want to go, now let's ask for a ticket.

Un billet pour + place + s'il vous plaît
(A ticket to + place + please)

eg: Un billet simple pour Metz, s'il vous plaît.
A single ticket to Metz, please

Un billet aller retour pour Amiens, s'il vous plaît.
A return ticket to Amiens please

You'll also need to know the following expressions:

un compartiment de deuxième classe	_a 2nd-class compartment_
fumeurs (m pl)	_smokers, smoking section of the train_
non-fumeurs (m pl)	_non-smokers, non-smoking section_

Le Billet — Ticket

S.N.C.F. BILLET
PARIS-LYON
LYON-PARIS
2ème classe
N'oubliez pas de composter ce billet
PRIX 600F
14/7/99   9h30

un billet simple	_single_
un billet aller retour	_return_
un billet de première classe	_a 1st-class ticket_

Les Arrivées et les Départs — Arrivals and Departures

À quelle heure arrive le train?
(What time does the train arrive?)

À quelle heure part le train?
(What time does the train leave?)

Remember the French use the 24-hour clock, so that 2pm becomes 14:00.

eg: Le train arrive à treize heures.   _The train arrives at 13:00 (1pm)_
Le train part à seize heures dix.   _The train leaves at 16:10 (4:10pm)_

Faut-il changer de train? — Must I change trains?

Oui, il faut changer de train.   Non, il ne faut pas changer de train.
Yes, you have to change trains   _No, you mustn't change trains_

Il faut changer de train à Bordeaux.

PARIS
Train direct.
BORDEAUX
MARSEILLE
PAU

Où est-ce qu'il faut changer pour + place?
(Where do I need to change for + place?)

eg: Il faut changer de train à Annecy.
You need to change trains at Annecy

Taking the Métro

Le Métropolitain — The Underground

The most famous '<u>métropolitain</u>' in France is the Paris Underground. Normally referred to as '<u>le métro</u>', it provides a quick and economical way of travelling around the capital.

un banc	bench	une station	station
un couloir	corridor	l'entrée (f)	entrance
un horaire	timetable	une ligne	line
un plan	map	la sortie	exit
un ticket	ticket	une zone	zone

un escalier	staircase
un escalier roulant	escalator
un tourniquet (-compteur)	turnstile
des renseignements	information
un carnet de tickets	book of tickets
une flèche de direction	direction arrow
des panneaux réclames (m pl)	billboards

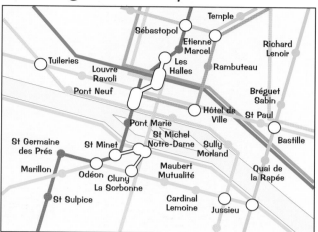

Pour Trouver La Station — Finding The Station

You're in Paris and want to see the sights but are having trouble finding the Underground station. Use this phrase:

Y a-t-il une station de métro près d'ici?

(Is there an Underground station near here?)

The answer will be something like this:

Oui, il y en a une là-bas/là-haut/à cent mètres d'ici.
Yes, there is one over there/up there/100 metres from here

> **Make sure that you know your directions — see P.67**

Acheter Les Tickets — Buying Tickets

If you're going to make a few journeys by Underground, buy a book of tickets, usually sold in tens. This works out a lot cheaper. Here's how to ask for tickets:

Je peux avoir un ticket pour + place + svp?

(May I have a ticket to + place + please?)

Je peux avoir un carnet de tickets svp?

(May I have a book of tickets please?)

If your journey is a long one you may need more than one ticket, or you can get an inter-zone ticket that lasts a whole day — <u>une carte d'abonnement</u>.

Les Avis — Signs and Notices to look out for

Animaux interdits	*No animals*
Défense de fumer	*No smoking*
Gardez votre billet	*Keep your ticket*
Défense de marcher sur les rails	*Do not walk on the tracks*
Attention aux voleurs à la tire	*Beware of pickpockets*
Compostez votre ticket	*Stamp your ticket*
Défense de déposer des ordures	*No littering*

Défense de fumer

Get it learned — don't get ideas above your station...

Loads of vocabulary here, but nicely broken into chunks. You need to be able to find the English words for the French phrase and vice-versa, so time to <u>cover</u> it up and <u>scribble</u> it out.

Bus and Air Travel

Getting around can be a real pain — especially all the vocab you've got to learn. So get going:

Aller en Autobus — Going by Bus

Vocabulaire:

- Le contrôleur (The inspector)
- L'autobus (m) (The bus)
- Le chauffeur (The driver)
- Le billet (The ticket)
- Le tarif (The fare)
- L'arrêt (m) d'autobus (The bus stop)

L'Arrêt d'Autobus — the Bus Stop

1) To ask where the stop is: **Où se trouve l'arrêt d'autobus?** (Where's the bus stop?)

2) You'll need to know if the bus is going your way:

Allez-vous à + place? (Are you going to + place?)

eg: *Allez-vous au marché central?*
Are you going to the central market?

Allez-vous à la gare?
Are you going to the train station?

> **REMEMBER** the forms of *à* with *le*,*la*,*l'* and *les*. If you are going to a specific place, eg: the central market, the station, the historical monuments etc., you will need them.

3) Once you are on the bus you'll need to pay, and to ask where you have to get off.

eg: *C'est combien le tarif?*　　　　*How much is the fare?*

Où est-ce que je descends pour + place?　　*Where do I get off for + place?*

4) Be prepared to act quickly — the answer to the last question could be:

eg: *Au prochain arrêt*　　　*At the next stop*

Les Avions — Aeroplanes

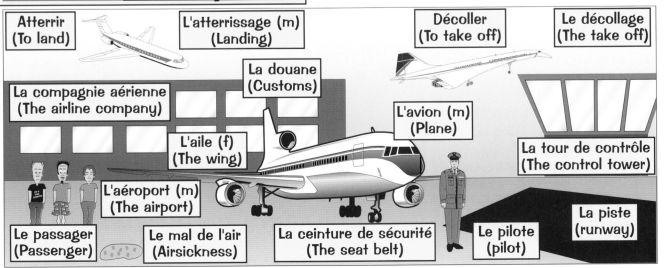

- Atterrir (To land)
- L'atterrissage (m) (Landing)
- Décoller (To take off)
- Le décollage (The take off)
- La douane (Customs)
- La compagnie aérienne (The airline company)
- L'avion (m) (Plane)
- La tour de contrôle (The control tower)
- L'aile (f) (The wing)
- L'aéroport (m) (The airport)
- La piste (runway)
- Le passager (Passenger)
- Le mal de l'air (Airsickness)
- La ceinture de sécurité (The seat belt)
- Le pilote (pilot)

Airport, Ferry and Hovercraft

Once you're in the airport the fun can really start — and don't forget your sea-travel vocab.

À l'Aéroport — At the Airport

You need to make sure you're on the plane when it leaves. Learn this well so you don't get left behind:

À quelle heure part-il?
(What time does it leave?)

À quelle heure arrive-t-il à + place?
(What time does it arrive at + place?)

Je voudrais réserver une place dans l'avion pour + place.
(I'd like to reserve a seat on the plane for + place.)

Paris
FRANCE
Marseille

Quelques Problèmes — Some Problems (You never know...)

Occasionally you may be delayed at the airport — you'll need to know what the announcements mean:

eg: Il y a du brouillard à Nantes — *It is foggy in Nantes*
Il neige à Lille — *It's snowing in Lille*
Le vol 276 a une heure de retard — *Flight 276 is one hour late*

Les Bateaux — Ships

le débarquement	disembarkation
débarquer	to disembark
l'embarquement	embarkation
embarquer	to embark

le bac	ferry
le bateau	boat
le navire	ship
le port	port

la mer	the sea
le mal de mer	seasickness
le passager piéton	foot passenger
la passerelle	footbridge
la traversée	crossing

Au Port — At the Port

Les Billets — Getting your Tickets

Deux billets pour Bastia s'il vous plaît. *Two tickets to Bastia please*

La Traversée — The Crossing

Quelle est la durée de la traversée, s'il vous plaît?
What is the duration of the crossing, please?
La traversée dure + deux heures/cinq heures/huit heures
The crossing takes + two hours/five hours/eight hours

L'Aéroglisseur — The Hovercraft

If you're not keen on long sea journeys, hovercraft can travel from England to France in just over half an hour!

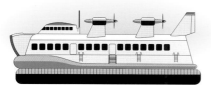

HOVERPORT DE CALAIS
CALAIS - DOUVRES
35 MINUTES
VISITEZ L'ANGLETERRE!

un coussin d'air	air cushion
un hovercraft	hovercraft
un hoverport	hoverport
le sable	sand
une vague	wave
la vitesse	speed

Learn your transport vocab — get a move on...

More vocabulary to learn, smashing... You'll need to be able to _understand_ the _announcements_ made at the airport as well as being able to book a ticket and ask what time a flight arrives.

Garage and Service Station

Time for some _driving vocab_ to finish the section — this could come up in role-plays so get learning.

Au Garage — At The Garage

l'accélérateur (m)	accelerator
l'embrayage (m)	clutch
le frein	brake
le moteur	engine
le pneu	tyre
le radiateur	radiator
les phares (m pl)	headlights
l'eau (f)	water
la panne	breakdown
la roue	wheel
la roue de secours	spare wheel
la voiture	car

Une Voiture En Panne

Ma Voiture!

Quelques Phrases Utiles — Some Dead Useful Phrases

Faites-vous des réparations?	Do you do repairs?
Ma voiture est en panne	My car has broken down
Pouvez-vous réparer les freins?	Can you repair the brakes?
Le/la/les + item + ne marche(nt) pas	The + item + does/do not work
Il faut remplacer le/la/les + item(s)	The + item(s) + must be replaced
Quel est le problème?	What is the problem?

Le pneu est crevé
The tyre is punctured

Combien de temps
faut-il attendre?
How long must I wait?

La Station-Service — The Service Station

You've stopped to buy petrol and oil and make sure the car's properly equipped for the journey ahead. Here's some key vocab:

l'arrosoir (m)	watering can
le magasin	the shop
le robinet	tap
la caisse	cash desk
l'essence (f)	petrol
l'huile (f)	oil
la pompe à essence	petrol pump
la pompe à pneus	air pump

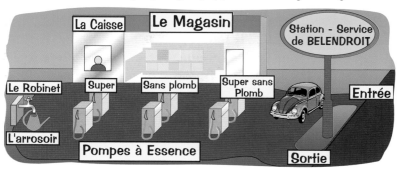

La Caisse — Le Magasin — Station - Service de BELENDROIT — Le Robinet — Super — Sans plomb — Super sans Plomb — Entrée — L'arrosoir — Pompes à Essence — Sortie

Sometimes you may need to ask the garage attendant (le pompiste) for what you need.

Un litre d'huile	A litre of oil
Faites-le plein	Fill the tank up
Vingt litres de super	20 litres of super (leaded)
Essence sans plomb	Unleaded petrol
Gonflez les pneus svp	Blow the tyres up please
Lavez le pare-brise svp	Wash the windscreen please
Je vous dois combien?	How much do I owe you?

Cars — they drive me round the bend..

This is the sort of thing that's not just useful in the Exams, but in real life, too. Vehicle problems and repairs could come up as a role play in the Speaking Exam — so learn it now, and be prepared. Time to _cover_, _scribble_ and _check_... There's still more important stuff to practise.

Revision Summary for Section Seven

Phew — another big section finished... I reckon it must be time for some more magic revision questions. Remember that the main thing here is practice. You really do have to keep going over the vocab and using it to answer questions. That's the only way you can get it sorted in your head, and the only way you can get yourself decent marks. So put a bit of effort in now and get these questions answered in French — you need to get them all right. And don't forget — there's no point in giving up, so keep going over them again and again. It's the only way...

1) How would you say that you want to be: a) a chef b) a fireman c) a musician?
2) How would you say that you work: a) in a bank b) in a travel agency c) in a factory?
3) How would you ask a French student what they want to do when they leave school?
4) What would you like to do when you leave school? Give three different answers.
5) What don't you want to be when you leave? Why?
6) How would you say you'd like to go to college and study: a) art b) psychology c) French?
7) What are the French names for: a) bakery b) bookshop c) perfumery d) fishmonger's?
8) You want to buy meat, fruit, medicine and paper but the supermarket is closed. Which shops should you go to instead? Answer in full sentences.
9) How would you ask for: a) six pens b) a dozen oranges c) 3 kilos of bananas d) two litres of milk e) 650g of raspberries?
10) You have just seen a thief in a department store and the detective is asking you to describe him — tell him he was wearing grey trousers, a blue pullover, black shoes, and green socks.
11) Leo has decided to get a new image to impress Kate, so he goes to the latest fashion store in town. How does he ask to try on the black suit? And the white trousers?
12) Leo has a new outfit but now he needs a present for Kate. How does he ask where the jewellery department is? And the record department?
13) Kate is still on holiday. She sees two signs. What do they mean: a) rabais b) liquidation?
14) How does Leo ask for a refund on his white trousers?
15) Dr. Frank N. Stein has decided to build a new Monster but he needs body parts. Name six important parts he needs for his creation.
16) How do you say: a) you have stomach ache b) you're cold c) you've broken your arm?
17) Dr. Frank N. Stein's Monster fell downstairs because the legs weren't properly fixed on. How does he ask at the chemist's for a plaster and some aspirin?
18) You are a doctor on call. How do you tell the patient to take the pills four times a day, before meals and before they go to bed?
19) Leo has decided to surprise Kate by going to meet her train in Paris. How does he ask for a single ticket to Paris? How does he ask if there's a non-smoking section?
20) Kate is getting ready to go home after her holiday. Jean-Claude takes her to the station. How does she ask what time her train leaves? How does she ask if she needs to change train?
21) Leo is in Paris. How does he ask where the underground is?
22) Kate arrives on the other side of Paris and decides to go and see the Eiffel Tower. How does she ask for a book of tickets on the underground?
23) Leo can't find the underground and he thinks that Kate has gone home. He decides to take a bus to the Eiffel Tower. How does he ask what the fare is? As the bus is going along, he sees Kate on the street. How does he ask to get off at the next bus stop?
24) How do you say: a) airline company b) runway c) customs d) landing?
25) How do you ask what time the plane leaves and what time it lands?
26) Ask how long the ferry crossing takes because you get seasick.
27) How do you say you've lost your wallet, your umbrella and your trousers?
28) The car breaks down. Tell the mechanic the tyre is punctured. Ask if he can fix the brakes.

The Countries of Europe

Get to know the names of _Countries_, _Continents_ and _Nationalities_ in French really well because you'll come across them in the _Reading_ and _Listening_ Papers. Feminine forms are in brackets.

Les Pays d'Europe — **The Countries of Europe**

Le Royaume Uni/Grande Bretagne

English	anglais(e)
Scottish	écossais(e)
Welsh	gallois(e)
Northern Irish	d'Irlande du Nord

Je suis né(e) en Écosse et je suis Écossais(e)
I was born in Scotland and I am Scottish

L'anglais est la langue commune à tous les pays du Royaume Uni.
English is the common language in the countries of the United Kingdom

Les Pays Francophones
— _French Speaking Countries_

French	français(e)
Belgian	belge
Swiss	suisse
Luxembourgian	luxembourgeois(e)

La Finlande
La Norvège
La Suède
L'Écosse
L'Irlande du Nord
Le Royaume Uni
Le Danemark
La Republique d'Irlande
L'Angleterre
La Belgique
L'Allemagne
La Pologne
Le Pays de Galles
Le Luxembourg
La Hongrie
La France
La Suisse
La Roumanie
L'Italie
L'Espagne
Le Portugal

On parle aussi l'italien et l'allemand en Suisse.
Italian and German are also spoken in Switzerland.

Je suis Belge et je parle français et flamand.
I am from Belgium and I speak French and Flemish.

Je suis Française et j'habite une des plus belles régions de la France, le Val de Loire.
I am French and I live in one of the most beautiful parts of France, the Loire Valley.

The other _Western European_ **countries**

allemand(e)	German	finlandais(e)	Finnish
portugais(e)	Portugese	danois(e)	Danish
espagnol(e)	Spanish	polonais(e)	Polish
italien(ne)	Italian	roumain(e)	Romanian
norvégien(ne)	Norwegian	hongrois(e)	Hungarian
suédois(e)	Swedish	grec(que)	Greek

Je suis Allemand et j'habite sur la frontière avec la France.
I am German and I live on the French frontier.

Je suis Italienne et j'habite à Rome, une des villes les plus historiques du monde.
I am Italian and I live in Rome, one of the most historic cities in the world.

Some of the Rest — _Asia_ **and the** _Americas_

La Chine	chinois(e)	_Chinese_	Les États Unis	americain(e)	_American_
Le Japon	japonais(e)	_Japanese_	Le Canada	canadien(ne)	_Canadian_
L'Inde	indien(ne)	_Indian_	Le Brésil	brésilien(ne)	_Brazilian_

Je viens du Canada. Au Canada, on parle le français et l'anglais. On est bilingue.
I come from Canada. In Canada we speak French and English. We are bilingual.

It's party time in Europe — Greece is the word...

The _key_ to nationalities is remembering your _masculine_ and _feminine_ forms — and don't forget that when you say you're a particular nationality it _doesn't_ have a _capital letter_, but country names _do_.

French Speaking Countries of the World

Due to France's colonial past, French is spoken in over _forty countries_ of the world.

The French Speaking Countries of the world — Africa

These countries are former French _colonies_. The countries of _North Africa_, i.e. _Morocco_, _Tunisia_ and _Algeria_, are particularly important, as many people have _emigrated_ from them to France — you could get asked about them in the _Speaking_ or _Listening_ papers.

A lot of the French speaking countries (_Francophone_) are still attached to France and called "_Départements d'Outre Mer_", like Réunion, La Nouvelle Caledonie etc.

Le Maroc · La Tunisie · L'Algerie · Le Continent d'Afrique · La Mauritanie · Le Mali · Le Niger · Le Senegal · Le Burkina Faso · Le Tchad · La Guinée · Le Bénin · La Côte d'Ivoire · Le Cameroun · Le Togo · Le Gabon · Le Rwanda · Le Zaire · Le Burundi · Le Congo · Madagascar · L'île Maurice

Other French Speaking Countries of the World

la Réunion, les Seychelles, la Polynésie Française (French Polynesia), la Guadaloupe et la Martinique, la Guyane Française (French Guyana), Haïti et la Nouvelle Calédonie (New Caledonia), le Vietnam, le Cambodge (Cambodia) et le Laos

Case Study — L'île Maurice

L'Histoire de l'île Maurice	History of Mauritius
Colonie de la France de 1715 à 1810. Colonie anglaise de 1910 à 1968.	It was a French colony 1715-1810. It was an English colony 1810-1968. It became independent in 1968.
Situation Géographique	**Geographical Situation**
Elle se trouve dans l'Océan Indien, près de l'Afrique du Sud, Madagascar et l'île de la Réunion, dans les tropiques.	It is in the Indian Ocean near South Africa, Madagascar and Reunion Island in the tropics.
La Population de l'île	**Population of the Island**
Elle a une population de plus d'un million. La population est multiraciale. Il y a des Hindous, des Chinois et des Créoles, et une minorité d'Européens.	There are over a million people. It is a multiracial country. The people are Hindus, Chinese, Creoles and a minority of Europeans.
Les Industries Principales	**Main Industries**
Le sucre, le tourisme et le textile	Sugar, tourism and textiles
Les Langues Parlées	**Languages**
Le français, l'anglais, le chinois, le créole, l'hindustani	French, English, Chinese, Creole and Hindi
L'Avenir de l'île	**Future of the Island**
Il semble prospère avec de nouvelles industries et presque pas de chômage	It seems prosperous with new industries and almost no unemployment

Maurice — funny name for an island...

The French Speaking World is pretty darn big... Remember — you could get asked about French material from _another country_, not just France. So learn the names — and where they are, too.

The Media

Examiners *love* these general discussion topics like the *media* — so don't forget to learn a few phrases so you can talk about how the media *affects your life*. Don't say I didn't warn you...

1) *Les Journaux et La Presse Écrite* — the Press

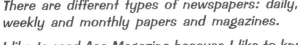

In France Le Figaro, Le Parisien and France Soir are "*de droite*" (right wing) and Libération is "*de gauche*" (left wing). Le Monde is "*indépendant*".

Quel genre de journal lis-tu? Des journaux nationaux ou régionaux?
What type of newspapers do you read? National or regional?

Je suis abonné à un journal à sensation.
I subscribe to a tabloid newspaper.

Il y a plusieurs types de journaux: des quotidiens, des hebdomadaires, des mensuels, et des magazines.
There are different types of newspapers: daily, weekly and monthly papers and magazines.

J'aime lire le Magazine Ace parce que j'aime connaître la vie et les opinions de mes chanteurs et mes acteurs préférés.
I like to read Ace Magazine because I like to know about the life and opinions of my favourite actors and singers.

2) *Going by the* Book

It's always good to be give *opinions* in the Speaking or Writing papers — so don't forget to learn these smashing examples and make up some of *your own*.

C'est un livre qui nous raconte la vie des jeunes d'aujourd'hui avec sensibilité — François Pasqua
It's a book which tells us about the life of today's young people with sensitivity — François Pasqua

C'est un livre merveilleux. On vit les mêmes tourments et les mêmes bonheurs des jeunes à la fin du 20ème siècle — Celine Dupont
It's a marvellous book. We experience the same worries and the same happiness of the young living at the end of the 20th century — Celine Dupont

3) *La Télévision/Le Petit Écran et la Radio*

Une chaîne de télévision/de radio — a TV/radio channel
Allumer la télévision — to turn the TV on
Éteindre la télévision — to switch the TV off
Le petit écran — the small screen (the television)

À la télévision je regarde les nouvelles. J'ai horreur des feuilletons. Mon émission préférée c'est les documentaires, les films d'aventure, les films policiers et les films du guerre.
On TV, I watch the news. I hate soaps. My favourite programmes are documentaries, adventure films, detective films and war films.

Ma soeur adore regarder les films d'amour.
My sister loves watching romantic films.

À la radio, j'écoute surtout la musique rap.
On the radio, I listen mainly to rap music.

J'aime les documentaires. Je m'intéresse surtout aux animaux.
I love documentaries. I'm mainly interested in animals.

L'émission préférée de mon frère est un feuilleton australien. Je trouve ça stupide et barbant.
My brother's favourite programme is an Australian soap. I find them stupid and boring.

It's too much — but that's entertainment...

Remember that if you say you like to watch TV in the Speaking exam, you'll *almost certainly* be asked to say *what* you like to watch — *learn it now*, and you won't be stuck for something to say. The stuff about the Press tends to come up in the Reading and Listening papers.

Advertising and Publicity

Advertising and publicity now rule the world. More important, you'll probably get an advert to write about in the _Reading_ paper and maybe the _Listening_, so make sure you read and listen _carefully_.

General Facts About Advertising

Where do we find it? Partout — Everywhere

Il y a des affiches dans les rues.
There are advertising posters in the streets.
La publicité est dans tous les lieux publics, les cinémas, les stades de foot, les magasins et les restaurants.
Advertising is in all public places, in cinemas, football stadia, shops and restaurants.

À la Télévision, la Radio, dans les Journaux
— On Television, Radio and in the Press

La publicité est essentielle aux chaînes commerciales de radio et télévision, dans les journaux et aux magazines.
Publicity is essential to commercial radio and television, newspapers and magazines.

Les entreprises, le gouvernement, les partis politiques, la police: tous utilisent la publicité.
Business, government, political parties, the police: all use advertising.

Publicité Informative et Nécessaire
— The Five Key Steps to Interpreting Adverts

MÉDECINS DE LA PAIX
Aujourd'hui en France, des milliers de jeunes sont en danger.

Avec un don de 100 F vous pouvez les aider
Avec un don de 100 F vous leur offrez des médicaments, des soins et de l'amitié

Nous les acceuillons, nous les écoutons, nous les soignons
Mais nous avons besoin de vous.
Alors faites un geste maintenant. Merci

This is an advert for a _Medical Organisation_ which cares for _young people_ living on the streets, asking for _Public Donations_.

Think about these points when you look at any advert:
1) Does the _picture_ give you a clue?
2) Is it written with '_tu_' or '_vous_'?
3) _REMEMBER:_ you don't need to understand every word to work out what it's about.
4) _Read through_ the text at least once _before_ you answer any _questions_.
5) Is it trying to make you _buy something_, or _offering_ you something 'cheap' or 'free', or _asking_ you to _do_ something?

Publicité Dangereuse — Dangerous Advertising

Advertising can have good and _bad points_ — you'll need to talk about both.

eg. cigarette advertising: Le gouvernement devrait l'interdire.
The government should ban it.

La publicité de la cigarette aux évènements sportifs est mauvaise pour les jeunes.
Cigarette advertising at sporting events is bad for young people.

"Exams are fun" — don't believe everything you read...
This is a topic that tends to come up in the Reading and Listening papers, where you've got to be able to _understand_ and _interpret_ an advert they give you, so get _practising_ right away.

Health and Life Style

Health is another one of those annoying _extended topics_ they like to get you to write about or talk about — the key to these is make sure you've got an _opinion_ and _plenty of vocab_ to use.

Quel est ton mode de vie? – What's your lifestyle like?

1) _La Nourriture_ — Food

Je mène une vie saine. Je fais des repas réguliers.
I have a healthy lifestyle. I eat regularly.

Je fais attention à ce que je mange. Je ne fais pas d'abus de graisse, de sucre ni de viande rouge.
I'm careful what I eat. I don't eat excess fat, sugar or red meat.

2) _Le Sport et les Exercices_ — Sport and Exercise

in
out
in
out

Pour me garder en forme, je fais régulièrement des exercices et du sport.
To keep in good shape, I exercise regularly and do sports.

Je fais du jogging et une fois par semaine je vais au centre sportif.
I go jogging and once a week I go to a sports centre.

3) _Combattre le Stress_ — Combating Stress

zzzzz

Pour combattre le stress, je dors huit heures par jour et j'ai des moments tranquilles pendant la journée.
To combat stress, I sleep eight hours a night and I have some quiet moments during the day.

Now things that are really bad for your health — _Les Choses Mauvaises pour la Santé_

Certaines Nourritures, _L'Alcool_, Les _Drogues_ et Les _Cigarettes_

Make use of expressions like:

On ne doit/devrait pas...   **Il ne faut pas + Infinitive**

On ne devrait pas fumer
One should not smoke

Il ne faut pas manger trop de graisse, trop de fast food.
One must not eat too much fatty food, too much fast food.

On devrait éviter les substances toxiques comme l'alcool et la drogue.
One should avoid toxic substances like alcohol and drugs.

The _reasons_ **why young people take** _drugs_ **and the** _consequences_

Pourquoi les jeunes d'aujourd'hui prennent-ils les drogues?
Why do young people today take drugs?

Ils disent qu'ils fument pour combattre le stress et pour faire comme leurs copains parce que c'est cool.
They say they smoke to combat stress and to be like their friends and because it's cool.

Est-ce que tu es de cet avis?   Quels sont les dangers de la drogue?
Do you agree with this?   _What are the dangers of drugs?_

Ils causent la dépendance, ce qui mène au crime et cause des maladies comme le cancer.
They cause dependency, and this leads to crime and causes diseases like cancer.

Stay smart, stay clean — drugs are for losers...

Young people's lifestyles are a topic examiners assume will _interest_ you. It often comes up in the Exams. So _learn_ this page, and _work out_ answers to some of the trickier questions in advance.

Social Issues

The _Environment_, _Pollution_ problems, _Recycling_, _Transport_, problems of the _Unemployed_ and the _Homeless_, _Crime_ — some more cheerful extended topics for discussion. It's got to be done!

1) La Pollution — Environmental Pollution

La pollution nous concerne tous, la pollution visible et invisible, la pollution de l'air, de l'eau et de la terre
Pollution is an issue which concerns us all, visible and invisible, the pollution of the air, water and earth

Le gouvernement fait-il assez pour combattre cette pollution?
Does the government do enough to combat this pollution?

Use the verb devoir in the conditional to say what the government and each individual should do to combat this

Le gouvernement devrait diminuer la circulation automobile dans les rues et développer les transports en commun
The government should reduce car traffic in towns and develop public transport

Il devrait encourager le recyclage des déchets
It should encourage recycling of waste materials

On devrait utiliser moins de plastique
One should use less plastic

On devrait penser plus à l'avenir de notre planète
We should think more about the future of our planet

2) L'Exclusion Sociale — Social Exclusion

Le chômage crée des inégalités sociales et il est la cause principale de l'exclusion
Unemployment causes social inequalities and is the main cause of exclusion

Il y a trop de jeunes et de moins jeunes qui sont sans domicile fixe
There are too many young and not so young homeless people

Ces jeunes quittent le foyer familial pour vivre dans les rues
These people leave their homes to live on the streets

Ils vivent en marge de la société
They live on the margin of society

Use these negative expressions to describe their situation

Ils n'ont aucun travail
They have no work

Ils n'ont rien à manger
They have nothing to eat

Ils n'ont ni argent ni domicile
They have no money and no home

3) Social Causes of Crime — Les Causes Sociales du Crime

La criminalité chez les jeunes touche tous les groupes sociaux
Crime amongst the young concerns all social classes

L'exclusion sociale est souvent la cause des problèmes des jeunes
Social exclusion is often the cause of problems of young people

Phew — more issues than the Beano...

This page gives you the _basic vocabulary_ to talk or write about all these problems. Remember, you have to be able to give _your opinion_ about subjects like this, so make sure you practise using these phrases. Start by scribbling a _mini-essay_ on the problems of the _Environment_.

Revision Summary for Section Eight

Loads to learn in this section — so you'd better get on with these fab revision questions. Remember to keep practising again and again until you've got every single one here learnt. The only way you'll get the marks is if you've prepared properly — and the best way to do that is to answer these questions in French. Some of these questions are fairly open-ended — you've really got to be able to give longer answers in the Exam too. So spend some time thinking about what you want to say before you answer them. Keep looking back over the section — you don't know exactly what'll come up in the Exam so you need to make sure you know it all. And if you don't get something first time around, then go back over it until you're absolutely sorted. So let's get going then.

1) How would you say that you come from Northern Ireland?
2) How would you say that you were born in Scotland?
3) What languages do they speak in Switzerland?
4) Name five Western European countries.
5) How would you say you are: a) Japanese b) American c) Brazilian?
6) How would you say that Canada is a bilingual country?
7) Name six French speaking countries around the World.
8) What do the French call a French speaking country?
9) Write a short paragraph on Mauritius giving five key facts about the country.
10) Your penfriend wants you to "éteindre la télévision". What must you do?
11) What is the French for: a) daily b) weekly c) monthly newspapers?
12) What kind of magazines do you like? Give reasons why.
13) Jean-Claude often wears black and has a goatee beard. He supports the parties on the political left wing. Which real French newspaper might he read? Why?
14) Give the name of a book you read recently, and two comments expressing what you thought of it. Answer in a full sentence.
15) What's French for: a) TV channel b) switch on the TV c) the small screen d) soap operas?
16) What kind of TV shows do you like to watch? Give at least two kinds, and explain why.
17) What kind of TV shows do you hate? Explain why.
18) What kind of music do you like to listen to?
19) Do you listen to the radio? Do you listen to a music station?
20) Where do we find a lot of advertising?
21) Write a paragraph giving five important facts about advertising. Do you think it is a good or a bad thing? Give your reasons why?
22) What do you do to relax? What do you do for exercise? How do you cope with stress?
23) What are the serious dangers of drugs? Why do you think people start taking them when they know the damage they can do? Give a detailed answer.
24) Write a paragraph giving four facts about pollution.
25) Is there a link between social exclusion and crime? Write a mini-essay explaining your opinion and the reasons why you believe it.
26) What do you think is the most serious problem affecting young people today? Give reasons for your answer.
27) If you could live in any country in the world, which country would you live in and why? Write a short paragraph explaining your reasons.
28) Kate is writing a letter to Leo. How would she say that she is from Belgium but she lives in England, that she likes watching soap operas and comedy shows on TV, and that she listens to cheesy pop music on the radio? How would she say that she is very worried about the environment in Europe, especially because of pollution from industry?

Asking Questions

OK then — it's time to revise some of the _key areas_ people get wrong in the Exams. _Question words_ are a really basic skill — so get this lot learned and get them right when you use them.

Est-ce que = Is...	Quand = When	Quel(le) = Which/What
Qu'est-ce que = What...	Comment = How	À quelle heure = At what time
Combien = How much	Qui = Who	Pourquoi = Why
Où = Where		Pour aller à = How do I get to

When to use these question words

1) **Est-ce que:**

   a) When a question in English starts with a verb, in French it starts with '_Est-ce que_' + _pronoun/noun + verb_. The verb may be in any tense.

   eg:

Est-ce que tu as des frères et des soeurs?	_(Present)_	_Do you have brothers and sisters?_
Est-ce qu'il est parti?	_(Past)_	_Has he left?_
Est-ce que tu iras en France l'été prochain?	_(Future)_	_Will you go to France next summer?_

   b) Sometimes French questions start with the pronoun or the noun — the subject — followed by the verb. The intonation of the sentence will tell you it's a question.

   eg:
   > Tu as des frères et des soeurs?
   > Il est parti?
   > Tu iras en France l'été prochain?

   c) Sometimes you can change the word order by putting the verb first, before the subject, and again without using est-ce que.

   eg:
   > As-tu des frères et des soeurs?
   > Est-il parti?
   > Iras-tu en France l'été prochain?

   You must practise _all three forms_ because you'll come across all of them in the Listening paper and you'll pick up loads of valuable marks if you use all three in the Speaking Exam.

2) **Qu'est-ce que:**

   It means '_what_'. Like 'est-ce que' it's followed by the _noun/pronoun + verb_.

   eg: _Qu'est-ce que_ vous désirez comme glace, Monsieur? _What ice cream would you like, Sir?_
   Qu'est-ce que vous avez comme parfums? _What flavours do you have?_

> **Est-ce que and Qu'est-ce que are the words most used by the French when they're asking questions and so they are the words the examiner will use most frequently**

3) **The rest** are easy to use because, just like their English versions, they are followed by _Verb + noun/pronoun_.

   eg: _Combien_ coûte un kilo de bananes svp?   _How much is a kilo of bananas please?_
   Où se trouve la gare svp?   _Where is the station please?_
   À quelle heure part le train pour Rouen?   _At what time does the Rouen train leave?_
   Pourquoi aimes-tu les maths?   _Why do you like maths?_

4) **Quel** _(Which/what)_ is followed immediately by a _noun_.

   eg: _Quel_ légume aimez-vous?   _What vegetable do you like?_

5) And last but not least: **Pour aller à...** _(How do I get to...)_ — for asking the way (see P.66-8)

Exam skills — a question of good revision...

Remember, there's _three_ ways to ask a question, and you do need to know them all. The question words are all important, so cover the page and list them all from memory. Then _learn_.

Answering Questions

Once you know about questions you've really got to _practise_ how to _answer_ them in detail. The Exam is about showing _how good_ you are at French — if you don't talk enough you can't do that.

1) _Always give as much_ Detail _as you can_

It's tempting to answer questions starting with "_Est-ce que_" simply "_Oui_" or "_Non_", but at Higher Level, you'll be expected to give _details_ after the "Oui" or "Non".

2) _Answer in the_ Correct Person _— Je or Nous_

When there's a _Tu_ in the question, you're being asked something personally so your reply should start with '_Je..._' Be careful — _Vous_ could be a formal question (reply with '_Je..._') or it could refer to _more than one person_ so your answer should start with '_Nous..._' And remember to put the verb in the right form!

Qu'est-ce que _vous_ désirez Mademoiselle? — What would you like Miss?
_Je_ voudrais un steak et des frites s'il vous plaît. — I would like a steak and chips please.

Qu'est-ce que _vous_ avez fait tes parents et toi? — What did you and your parents do?
Nous sommes allés en France. — We went to France.

3) _The_ Tense _Of the Verb is_ the Same _in the Answer as the Question_

Pay attention to the _tense_ of the verb in the question, as you must reply in the _same_ tense.

eg: Qu'est-ce que tu feras après l'école? — What will you do after school?
J'irai à l'université. — I shall go to University.
The verbs in the question and the answer are both in the FUTURE

Est-ce-que le train est parti? — Has the train left?
Oui, il est parti. — Yes it has left.
The verbs in the question and the answer are both in the PAST

The same rule applies for questions starting with _comment_, _quand_, _quel_, _où_, _pourquoi_, _à quelle heure_. You must know what they all mean.

4) _Use The_ Same Verb _as in the_ Question

Practise _recognising_ the verbs in the question so that you have no difficulty using the _same verb_ to answer.

BUT — be careful if the verb FAIRE is in the question! You'll definitely need to answer using a different verb

eg: Qu'est-ce que tu _feras_ plus tard dans la vie? — What will you do for a career?
Je _serai_ médecin/professeur/avocat etc... — I will be a doctor/teacher/lawyer etc...

5) _Prepare_ Answers to the _Obvious Questions_

Think of answers for typical questions like: "Qu'est-ce que tu vas faire après les examens?" (What are you going to do after the exams?). The answer to any question with "_Pourquoi?_" (Why?) should always begin "_Parce que ...._" (Because....).

Let me guess — you want some answers...

Here are the _five main points_ to bear in mind when _answering questions_. Remember, in the Oral Exam you'll be asked "Pourquoi?" a lot, so practise the _reasons_ why you like or don't like stuff.

Formal Letters

You'd have to write formal letters to make a _request_ or express _apologies_ or _thanks_. You need to learn a few expressions and use them in the appropriate context. _Easy to learn_ and _easy to use_.

Writing Formal Letters is simple— just Follow the Rules

1) Use the set layout and begin properly:

Do _not_ write _Cher/Chère_ Monsieur/Madame (Dear Sir/ Madam) as you would in English. The French use "Cher" to address _only_ those people who are dear to them, i.e. members of _family_, _friends_ and _acquaintances_.

> 10 Honeysuckle Close
> Kingston upon Thames
> Surrey 3KT 5SL
> Le 10 mai 1998
>
> Monsieur/Madame,

2) Get to the purpose of your letter right away

Lettre à un Syndicat d'Initiative

> J'ai l'intention de passer une semaine à Bordeaux cet été et je voudrais avoir une liste d'hôtels à deux étoiles et des renseignements sur les lieux à visiter.

Letter to a Tourist Office

> _I intend to spend a week in Bordeaux this summer and I would like to have a list of two star hotels and information on places to see._

3) You make your request

> Pourriez-vous m'envoyer une liste d'hôtels et un dépliant sur la région de Bordeaux s'il vous plaît? Je vous en serais reconnaissant(e).

> _Could you please send me a list of hotels and a leaflet on Bordeaux please? I would be most grateful._

4) You end your letter politely

> Je vous prie d'agréer, Monsieur/Madame, l'expression de mes sentiments distingués.

Bordeaux
AQUITAINE
Spain

> _Yours sincerely_
> (2 _words_ in English, 2 _lines_ in French!)

5) You sign your name and surname legibly

There are various contexts they'll use in the Exam to get you to write a letter. Learn the ones below:

Pour réserver une chambre/un emplacement — To book a room/a place

> Je voudrais réserver une chambre/un emplacement du 16 au 20 juillet pour quatre nuits. Pourriez-vous me donner des renseignements sur le prix des chambres/d'un emplacement....

> I would like to book a room/a site from 16-20 July for four nights. Could you please give me some information on the price of rooms/a site.

Comment s'excuser — How to apologise

You may have to apologise for something, or for leaving something in a hotel room:
"_Je regrette de vous informer que..._" (I am sorry to inform you that...) and finish your letter with "_Je vous prie d'accepter mes excuses._" and with the formal ending.

Pour demander un emploi — To apply for a job

1) Je vous écris au sujet de votre annonce dans Le Figaro du.... (+ DATE)
   I am writing in response to your advertisement in Le Figaro of..... (+ DATE)
2) Je vous écris pour vous demander des renseignements sur les possibilités de travailler dans votre compagnie.
   I am writing to find out the possibilities of working with your Company.

Then give a description of your education, your personality and when you would be able to start.

Pour remercier pour une lettre — To thank for a letter

Writing in reply to a formal letter always starts with "_Je vous remercie de votre lettre du..._" (Thank you for your letter of...) + DATE. _Don't forget to end with the proper ending! (see above)_

Just learn the rules — the letter of the law...

Lots of lovely _rules_ to follow. You really do need to learn the correct way to finish a letter _off by heart_. Learn all the different letters on this page, you could be asked to write _any_ of them...

Letters to Friends

You're more than likely to be asked to _write_ to your _penfriend_ either in reply to his/her letter or to write and tell them or ask them something. These are easy marks if you learn the tricks.

Informal Letters _are easy too — just_ Follow the Formula

1) The layout — Town, Date and Cher:

You don't need your address in an informal letter, just the town and the date on the top right hand corner of the page.

Usually French people start their informal letters with _Cher..._

> Kingston, le 12 mai
>
> Cher Paul/Chère Céline,
>   merci de ta lettre, comment
>   vas-tu? Moi je vais bien et

2) Thank him/her for the letter, and ask how he/she is...

Tell him/her about yourself and your family and say you hope that his/her family are well too.

Merci de ta lettre. Comment vas-tu? Moi, je vais bien et la famille aussi. J'espère que tout le monde va bien chez toi.	_Thank you for your letter. How are you? As for me I am well and my family too. I hope that your family is well too._

3) Now the body of the letter:

Make sure you tell him/her everything he/she has asked:

Tu m'as demandé dans ta lettre ce que... Eh bien voilà...
You've asked me in your letter what... Well, here you are...

If he/she's told you about a French custom or something is done in France which we don't do in England you can say:

Chez nous, ce n'est pas comme ça.
In England, it is not like this

Make sure you answer _every single one_ of his/her _questions_.

> **Use all you've learnt about _comparatives_ (see P.7). Examiners like to see you using the grammar which you've learnt. So a lot of "_plus_" and "_moins_" will earn you _marks_.**

4) If you are writing to ask him/her something, you say:

Est-ce que tu peux me dire ce que... (Can you tell me what...)

or

Qu'est-ce que tu penses de... (What do you think of...)

You may have to ask him/her what he/she thinks of things like pop music, sports, friends...
Study the "Asking Questions" page so that you've got plenty of ideas.

5) Now to close your letter:

"Maintenant, je dois terminer ma lettre"   _Now I must end my letter_
"Je dois faire mes devoirs"   _I must do my homework_
 or "Je dois aider ma mère"   _I must help my mother_

Ask him/her to write to you soon:
"Écris-moi bientôt" or "Donne-moi vite de tes nouvelles" _(Write to me quickly)_

6) Now to sign off. The French have various ways of ending a letter. Use one of these:

| Amicalement | Ton ami/amie | Toutes mes amitiés | (followed by your name) |

What do you call medieval letters — chain mail...

Here's a simple _six step recipe_ to write a nice chatty letter. Remember, if you use plenty of the _grammar skills_ you've been learning along the way, you can pick up a lot of _marks_ here...

Faxes, Phones and e-mails

Yep, we're in the age of modern technology now, and you'll really pick up marks if you know about these skills. You might even get a job because of them...

Faxes and E-mails are a Quick Way of Sending a letter

Here's what a fax looks like:

> **The Whitehart Hotel**
> **Tel: 0181 255 505**
>
> REF: JS/WB1   (ref based on the person sending it and the person typing it)
> DATE: 12 août 2000
>
> Envoi de: James Sanders   (sent by James Sanders)
> À l'attention de: Monsieur Pierre Dupont (For the attention of Mr P Dupont)
> Numéro de Fax: 1329   (Fax no. 1329)
> Nombre de pages: 1   (No. of pages: 1)
> Y compris page de couverture   (Front page included)
>
> Message: (Your message)
> Suite à votre fax du 11 août nous confirmons la réservation d'une chambre à un lit avec salle de bains pour une personne pour les nuits du 10 et 11 septembre 1998. Prix de la chambre £40.00 par nuit avec petit déjeuner.
>
> *JSSanders*

(Further to your fax of 11 August, we confirm the booking of one single room with bathroom for the nights of 10 and 11 September 1998. Price of room £40.00 per night with continental breakfast.)

Here's how the same information would be given by e-mail:

> e-mail   ✕
> Sujet: (subject) Confirmation de réservation de chambre (confirmation of room booking)
> Date: vendredi 12 août 1998 11:50:26 (Date and time)
> De: James Sanders + e-mail address   (From ...)
> À: Pierre Dupont + e-mail address   (To ...)
> Message: Nous confirmons la réservation d'une chambre à un lit avec salle de bains pour une personne pour les nuits du 10 et 11 septembre 1998. Prix de la chambre £40.00 par nuit avec petit déjeuner.

Using the Telephone

1) Someone answering the phone in a French company would say the name of the company, followed by "*Bonjour*". A French person answering the phone in their house would say "*Allô*".

2) The person calling should then give their name, and if the phonecall is a professional one, their company: "Ici c'est Pierre Leroi, de Renault. Je voudrais parler à Monsieur Lafitte s'il vous plaît"
    This is Pierre Leroi from Renault. I would like to speak to Mr Lafitte please

3) If the person is not there, the telephonist will say:
    "Je suis désolé mais Monsieur Lafitte n'est pas là. Voulez-vous lui laisser un message?"
    I am sorry but Mr Lafitte is not in. Would you like to leave a message for him?

4) If he is in, the telephonist will say: "Un moment monsieur, je vous le passe"
    Just a minute sir, I'll put him through

Phones and e-mail — learn the basic fax...

If you're asked to write a fax or an e-mail, it's got to be to be _short_ and to the _point_. Don't forget, though, your _grammar_ still needs to be _spot-on_. Learn and practise the proper phrases.

98

Writing an Essay

This is a pretty nasty part of the Exam — but don't worry, just learn these simple rules and be careful with your _grammar_.

In an Essay you'll have to do _one_ of these _four things_:

> 1) **Give some facts and give your opinion on them**
> 2) **Give an account of something you did**
> 3) **Talk about something you will, or intend, to do**
> 4) **Talk about something you would like to do**

Here's all you need to know

TENSES: You must know what _tense_ you're going to write the essay in (_past, present_ or _future_). The examiners are testing your ability to write a _coherent_ piece in French showing that you've mastered the _basic structure_ of the language, especially the _verbs_.

1) Let's look at the _facts_: What are the _facts_ that you need to know? — things about _yourself_, your _school_, your _family_, your _friends_, your _town/village_, your _country_ and its _customs_ and things that concern _people of your age_.

> **If you are asked about any of these topics you must use the present tense**

Use it with a variety of _regular_, _irregular_ and _reflexive_ verbs, plus a range of French expressions.

Dans ma famille nous sommes quatre personnes.	_There are four of us in my family._
Ma ville se trouve dans le sud de l'Angleterre.	_My town is situated in the south of England._
Il n'y a rien à faire dans mon village.	_There's nothing to do in my village._

When you are answering a letter from your penfriend and you're telling him/her about your school, your town or your village, make sure you use a lot of _adjectives_ and _adverbs_.

Mon école est formidable. Il y a des choses intéressantes à faire dans ma ville.	_My school is great. There are interesting things to do in my town._

2) Giving an _account_ of... something _you did_ or something that _happened_ in the not too _distant past_, or something you _witnessed_. This essay could be in the form of a _letter_ or a _narrative_. Here of course, the examiner is testing your _knowledge_ and _use_ of the _past tense_.

Use the _Perfect_ and _Imperfect_ tenses. Show you know the difference between the two — the imperfect _setting the scene_ in the past, and the perfect _describing an action_ that took place in the past and is _now over_. You'll need a variety of verbs, using either '_avoir_' or '_être_' as auxiliaries. Don't forget the use of _reflexive_ verbs in the past and the use of pronouns other than Je.

Nous avons fait une promenade en voiture.	_We went for a drive in the car._
Nous nous sommes bien amusés.	_We had a good time._

3) Now about things you _intend_ or _are going_ to do: Here remember to use the _Future_ tense throughout and to use _Aller (in the present tense)_ + _an Infinitive_. Again, use a range of regular and irregular verbs. Learn how to say things which you intend to do after your GCSE's or A-levels. Remember the use of "_J'ai l'intention de_" + INFINITIVE (_I intend to_), "_D'abord_" (_first of all_) and "_Ensuite_" (_then_).

4) Finally about things you _would like_ to do: In this case you need to use the conditional:

Je voudrais aller à l'université.	_I would like to go to university._
Je voudrais être médecin.	_I would like to be a doctor._

Writing is like swordfighting — get to the point...

Another big scary exam topic made simple. It's really all down to a bit of _planning ahead_. Remember, you've got to cover everything you've been asked in a mere 150 words, which _isn't a lot_. Don't waste words on irrelevant information — answer the question you're given.

Useful Phrases to Impress the Examiner

Phew — here are some smashing phrases for you to learn and stick in your essays. These are dead useful for picking up high marks — so make sure you learn the right forms and use them properly.

Essay Phrases that use the Present Tense

1) Show the examiner how <u>wide</u> your <u>vocabulary</u> is by using expressions like these:

d'habitude / normalement	*usually*		quelquefois	*sometimes*
une fois par mois	*once a month*		la plupart du temps	*most of the time*
assez souvent	*often*			

Je fais du tennis <u>une fois par semaine</u> — *I play tennis once a week*
<u>D'habitude</u> je fais mes devoirs en rentrant de l'école — *Normally I do my homework when I get home from school*
Très <u>souvent</u> j'aide ma mère à faire la vaisselle — *I often help my mother with the washing up*

2) Expressions with the verb "<u>Faire</u>" are always winners with examiners. If at all possible use the expression "<u>cela fait</u>" + *specific amount of time* + <u>que</u>.
<u>Cela fait</u> quatre ans <u>que</u> je joue du piano — *I have been playing the piano for four years*

3) Expressions with "<u>Il faut</u>" and "<u>On doit</u>" are very good:
Dans mon école <u>il faut/on doit</u> porter un uniforme — *At my school we must wear a uniform*

4) Expressions with "<u>On peut</u>" are useful too:
Dans ma ville <u>on peut</u> faire du patin à glace — *In my town we can go ice skating*

5) Examiners like to see the use of an <u>Infinitive</u> either directly after the verb or with <u>à</u> and <u>de</u>.
J'adore <u>faire</u> <u>de</u> l'équitation — *I love horse riding*
J'apprends <u>à jouer</u> aux échecs en ce moment — *I am learning to play chess*

6) And they particularly like to see the use of <u>Avant de</u> + *infinitive* and <u>Venir de</u> + *infinitive*.
<u>Avant d'aller</u> à l'école, je prends mon petit déjeuner — *Before going to school, I have breakfast*
Je <u>viens de</u> voir ce film — *I have just seen this film.*

For Essays where you need the Past Tense

1) Use expressions like <u>l'année dernière/l'été dernier</u> (*last year/summer*) and <u>il y a un an</u> / <u>deux ans</u> (*a year ago/two years ago*):
<u>L'année dernière</u> je suis allé en vacances en France — *Last year I went on holiday to France*
<u>Il y a deux semaines</u> j'ai oublié mon pantalon — *Two weeks ago I forgot my trousers*

2) Another favourite is <u>Après avoir</u> + *past participle* (*after having done something*):
<u>Après avoir</u> <u>acheté</u> mon billet je suis monté dans le train — *Having bought my ticket I boarded the train*

3) At higher level you must be able to use the <u>Past</u> in conjunction with the <u>Imperfect</u>:
Notre hôtel <u>était</u> à quelques mètres de la plage et nous <u>avons pu</u> beaucoup nager — *Our hotel was a few metres from the beach and we were able to swim a lot*

4) Use <u>Idiomatic Expressions</u> like:
Nous nous sommes bien amusés — *We had a very good time*
Nous avons pris l'avion/nous avons voyagé en avion — *We travelled by plane*

For Essays requiring the use of the Future

Use <u>quand</u> and <u>lorsque</u> to make complex sentences:

<u>Quand</u> je terminerai mes études, je ferai des recherches scientifiques. *When I finish my studies, I shall do scientific research*

Note the use of the future with <u>both</u> verbs in French

<u>Lorsque</u> j'aurai dix-huit ans, je prendrai des leçons de conduite. *When I am 18 I'll have driving lessons*

Tenses — dunno if I'm coming or I'm going or I've been...

You've learnt your <u>present</u>, <u>past</u> and <u>future</u> tenses in Section One, and now the time comes to make <u>full use</u> of them with these smart little phrases. At the end of the day, it'll get you <u>marks</u>.

More Useful Phrases

Almost there — but this *everyday French* is the key to sounding good in the Oral. So get *revising*.

1) Information you ask a Passer-By

Is there/ Are there any...in this town   *Est-ce qu'il y a ... dans cette ville*
Excuse me, I am looking for...   *Excusez moi, je cherche...*

Where can I buy stamps   *Où puis-je acheter des timbres s'il vous plaît?*
At what time does the shop open?   *À quelle heure s'ouvre le magasin?*
What are the opening hours?   *Quelles sont les heures d'ouverture?*

Can you please help me?   *Est-ce que vous pouvez m'aider?*   Where is...?   *Où se trouve...?*
How can I get to..?   *Pour aller à la/au...?*   Is it near/far from here?   *Est-ce que c'est près/loin d'ici?*

2) Things you ask for in a Shop, Restaurant, Train Station etc.

How much is..?   *Combien coûte?*   Can I please have..?   *Est-ce que je peux avoir...?*
How much is all this?   *Ça fait combien?*   Does it go to/stop at?   *Est-ce qu'il va à/ s'arrête à*
Do you have...   *Est-ce que vous avez...*   What is...like?   *Comment est...?*

What sort of...do you have/is there   *Qu'est-ce que vous avez comme/Qu'est-ce qu'il y a comme...*
Give me this one please   *Donnez-moi celui-ci s'il vous plaît*   I would like...   *J'aimerais/je voudrais...*

3) Things you discuss with your Penfriend

Do you have...?   *Est-ce que tu as...?*   Do you go to..?   *Est-ce que tu vas au/à la...?*
What do you do...?   *Qu'est-ce que tu fais...?*   How about going to...   *Si on allait à...*
What sort of...do you like/prefer?   *Qu'est-ce que tu aimes/préfères?*
How about having a game of...   *Si on jouait au...*
What is the weather forecast like?   *Quelles sont les prévisions de la météo?*
What's on TV tonight?   *Qu'est-ce qu'on passe à la télé ce soir?*

4) For day-to-day Conversation with your Hosts in France

Use the verb Faire to talk about the weather
Il fait beau n'est-ce pas?
The weather is nice isn't it?

Use the verb Avoir to say what's wrong with you
J'ai froid/chaud/soif/peur/besoin de/envie de
I am cold/hot/thisty/frightened/I need/want

Use the verb Pouvoir to ask whether you can help
Est-ce que je peux vous aider à + infinitive   *Can I help you to...*
Est-ce que je peux mettre la table?   *Can I lay the table?*
Est-ce que je peux faire la vaisselle?   *Can I do the washing up?*

Use the verb Devoir to ask what you have to do...
Est-ce que je dois prendre un pull?   *Do I need to take a pull over?*
Est-ce que je dois porter mon passeport?   *Do I need to take my passport?*

5) For chatting to your Penfriend when he/she visits you

Est-ce que tu aimes la nourriture anglaise?   *Do you like English food?*
Est-ce que tu voudrais... + infinitive   *Would you like to...*
Est-ce que le film t'a plu?   *Did you like the film?*   *Est-ce que tu préférerais...*   *Would you prefer to...*

6) Other Useful Phrases

Quelle horreur = *How dreadful*   *Je suis désolé(e)* = *I am sorry*   *Peut-être* = *Maybe*
Que faire? = *What shall we do?*   *Heureusement* = *Luckily*   *Quelle chance* = *How lucky*

I like a nice chat — a chien isn't bad either...

This is the really exciting bit. Things that'll make you sound almost like a *real French person*. And get you *top marks*. This sort of thing is very useful for situations like visiting your penfriend or if he/she comes to stay — it's not *all* exam, exam, exam here, you know, it just *mostly* is...

Revision Summary for Section Nine

All over — well almost. But first you need to finish off with these outrageously awesome revision questions — it's for your own good. Remember — the key for the Exams is to have lots of ideas learned in advance, and lots of vocabulary so that you'll always have something to say. Don't forget to keep your French clear and think about what the questions are asking you. Loads of easy marks get wasted every year when people don't read the questions. So take your time now and get this stuff learned — and when the Exams come around, you'll be sorted. Good luck.

1) You have a new penfriend. How would you ask them: a) how they are b) what they do in their spare time c) whether they have brothers and sisters? For part c) give three different way of asking the question.
2) How would you ask the waiter in a restaurant what type of ice cream they serve?
3) How would you ask a ticket collector what time the train arrives in Amiens?
4) How would you ask a passer-by how to get to the town hall?
5) Give a list of five things you like to do in your spare time.
6) Kate has won a competition to interview her idol, Ronan, the lead singer of her favourite band the Condiment Boyz. She is worried she will get overexcited so you need to help her with questions. How would she ask: a) whether he has any younger brothers b) why he likes his job c) where he can be seen in concert d) what his plans for the future are?
7) How would Ronan tell Kate that: a) he has two younger brothers b) he likes singing and meeting people c) he's touring Britain next year d) he'd like to learn to read music?
8) What are the three rules of person, tense and verb for answering questions? Give your answer in English. What is different about questions with the verb faire?
9) What are the five rules of writing formal letters? Answer in English.
10) You are writing a formal letter to the Tourist Office in the Alps asking for information about hotels during the winter months. Ask about cheap hotels and the best places to go for skiing. Thank them for their time and for the information.
11) You are writing a formal letter to the Ski Hotel in Chamonix.   Ask if you can reserve a room for two people for one week from 9-16 January. Ask for a full list of room prices. Ask whether breakfast is included in the price. Thank them and say you look forward to seeing them soon.
12) The Condiment Boyz' manager Bryan is writing a letter of apology to a hotel in Paris after Ronan damaged some furniture one evening. How would he apologise for TV set being broken? How would he apologise for Ronan being rude to the manager? How would he end the letter offering to pay for the damage and inconvenience?
13) You are applying for a job as an office assistant with Le Figaro newspaper. Write a brief letter of application explaining who you are and why you would be good at the job and telling them you could start as soon as they wanted. Remember to sell yourself.
14) Write a letter to your new penfriend, telling them about yourself, your family and your home town. Ask about their lives: their family and friends, what they do for fun and what they think of school. Use at least ten different phrases and close the letter.
15) Kate is sending an e-mail to Leo. How does she tell him she will be home from the competition trip soon? How does she say she is missing him? How does she say Ronan is taking her to the Condiment Boyz concert for free? How does she say she hopes Leo's exam went OK?
16) What are the four key factors in essay writing? Answer in English.
17) Write a short essay on your favourite hobby using as many phrases and verb tenses as you can. You should write at least 300 words.
18) Kate has returned home and goes to meet Leo after his French exam. How does she wish him luck with the results?

French-English Dictionary

This dictionary is based on the vocabulary requirements of all Examining Boards. It contains loads of top useful words, as well as tricky words that no one ever explains. You can look things up in the index to find out more on any particular subject. *m* indicates a masculine noun, *f* a feminine noun, and *pl* a plural noun. *m/f* means the noun can be made masculine or feminine without changing spelling.

A

à   at, in, to
à coté de   beside
à droite/gauche   on the right/left
à mon avis   in my opinion
à pied   on foot
acheter   to buy
addition *f*   bill
adorer   to like (a lot)
affaires *fpl*   business
agréable   pleasant, nice
aider   to help
aimer   to like, to love
alimentation *f*   food
aller   to go
aller-retour   return (ticket)
aller-simple   single (ticket)
alors   then, so, well
ami(e)   friend
amusant   funny, enjoyable
amuser – s'amuser
      to enjoy oneself
an *m*, année *f*   year
anniversaire *m*   birthday
août *m*   August
apprendre   to learn
après(-midi) *m or f*   after(noon)
arbre *m*   tree
argent *m* (de poche)
      (pocket) money
arrêt d'autobus *m*   bus stop
arriver   to arrive
aspirateur *m*   vacuum cleaner
assez   enough
assiette *f*   plate
attendre   to wait
au moins   at least
au revoir   goodbye
au secours!   help!
aujourd'hui   today
aussi   also
autocar *m*   coach
autoroute *f*   motorway
autre   other
avant   before
avec   with
avion *m*   aeroplane
avis *m*   opinion
avoir (besoin de)
      to have (to need)
avril *m*   April

B

banlieue   outskirts
banque *f*   bank
bateau *m*   boat
bâtiment *m*   building
bavarder   to chat
beau   fine, attractive
beaucoup   a lot, much
bébé *m*   baby
bien   well
bientôt   soon
bienvenu(e)   welcome
billet *m*   ticket
blanc(he)   white
bleu(e)   blue
boire, boisson *f*   to drink, a drink
boîte *f*   box
bon   good
bon marché   cheap
bonjour   good morning/afternoon
bonne chance   good luck
bonne nuit   good night
bonsoir   good evening
bord *m* de la mer   the seaside
boum *f*   party
bouteille *f*   bottle
bras *m*   arm
brosse à dents *f*   tooth brush
brouillard *m*   fog
bruit *m*   noise
brun   brown
bureau *m* (de poste)   (post) office

C

ça   that, it
ça va   OK, alright
cadeau *m*   present
cahier *m*   exercise book, jotter
campagne *f*   countryside
car   because, since
carrefour *m*   crossroads
carte postale *f*   postcard
ce, cet, etc.   this, these
ceci, cela   this one, that one
célèbre   famous
cent   one/a hundred
centime *m*
      a hundredth of a Franc
c'est   it/this is
c'était   it/this was
chambre *f*   bedroom
chance *f*   luck

changer   to change
chanson *f*   song
chanter/chanteur   to sing/singer
charmant   charming
chaud   hot
chèque de voyage *m*
      traveller's cheque
cher   dear, expensive
cheveux *mpl*   hair
chez moi/toi   my/your house
chips *fpl*   crisps
choisir   to choose
chômage *m*   unemployment
chose *f*   thing
coeur *m*   heart
coin *m*   corner
combien   how much
comme   like, as
comment   how
complet *m*, complète *f*   full
comprendre   to understand
compris   included
connaître   to know, understand
conseiller   to advise
content   happy
contraire *m*   opposite
contre   against
copain *m*, copine *f*   friend
correspondant(e)   penfriend
côte *f*   coast
côté *m*   side, way
couleur *f*   colour
cours *m*   lesson
cuir   to cook

D

d'abord   first, to begin with
d'accord   OK, agreed
dangereux   dangerous
dans   in, into, to, inside
de   of, from, by
de rien   don't mention it
de temps en temps
      from time to time
décembre *m*   December
décider   to decide
défense de (fumer)
      (smoking) forbidden
déjeuner *m*   lunch
délicieux   delicious
demain   tomorrow
demander   to ask

French-English Dictionary

demi   half
dépliant *m*   leaflet, brochure
depuis   since, for, from
dernier   last
derrière   behind
descendre
       to go down, to get down
désirer   to desire, to want
désolé   sorry
dessin *m*   drawing
détester   to hate
deuxième   second
devant   before
devoir, devoirs
       to have to, homework
d'habitude   usually
difficile   difficult
dimanche *m*   Sunday
dîner   evening meal
dire   to say
donc   therefore, so
donner   to give
dormir   to sleep
douche *f*   shower
dur   hard, difficult
durer   to last

E

eau *f* (potable)
       (drinking) water
école *f*   school
écouter   to listen
écrire   to write
élève *m/f*   student, pupil
emploi *m*   job
en   on, in, into, by, of them
en bas/haut   at the bottom/top
en panne   broken down
en retard   late
encore   more, yet
enfant *m/f*   child
ennuyeux   boring
ensuite   then, next
entendre   to hear, understand
entre   between
entrée *f*   entrance, starter
environ   about, roughly
envoyer   to send
espérer   to hope
essayer   to try
est   is, east
est-ce que   is...?
et   and
être   to be
étudier   to study
eux   they, them
examen *m*   exam

exemple *m*   example
expliquer   to explain
extrait *m*   extract

F

facile   easy
facteur/facteuse
       postman/postwoman
faible   weak
faim - j'ai faim   I'm hungry
faire   to do
famille *f*   family
fatigué   tired
faux   false
femme *f*   woman/wife
fermé   closed
feu *m* (feux d'artifice)
       fire (fireworks)
février *m*   February
fille *f*   girl, daughter
fils *m*   son
fois *f*, une fois   time, once
fort   strong
franc *m*   French unit of currency
frère *m*   brother
froid - j'ai froid   cold - I'm cold
fumer   to smoke

G

garçon *m*   boy, waiter
gare *f*   train station
gauche   left
gentil   kind, nice
grand   big, tall, great
gratuit   free
gris   grey
gros   large, fat
guichet *m*   ticket office

H

habiter   to live in
heure *f*   hour
heureux   happy
hier   yesterday
homme *m*   man
hôpital *m*   hospital
horaire *m*   timetable

I

idée *f*   idea
il faut   you must, one has to
il n'y a pas   there isn't/aren't
il y a   there is, there are
il y aura/avait   there will be/were
immeuble *m*   building
inclus   included, inclusive
interdit   forbidden
inviter   to invite

J, K

jamais   never
janvier *m*   January
jaune   yellow
jeu *m* - jeu d'échecs
       game - chess set
jeudi *m*   Thursday
jeune   young
jouer   to play
jour *m*   day
journal *m*   newspaper
juin *m*   June
juillet *m*   July
jusqu'à   until

L

là-bas   over there
laisser   to leave
langue *f*   tongue, language
laver   to wash
le / la / les / l'   the
lentement   slowly
leur   their, them
lever - se lever   to get up
libre   free, available
lire   to read
lit *m*   bed
livre *m* (sterling)
       pound (sterling)
loin de   far from
loisir *m*   pastime
lundi *m*   Monday
lunettes *fpl*   glasses
lycée *m*   secondary school

M

madame *f*   madam, Mrs.
mademoiselle *f*   Miss
magasin *m*   shop
mai *m*   May
maintenant   now
mairie *f*   town hall
mais   but
maison *f*   house
mal   badly, pain
malade   ill
manger   to eat
marché *m*   market
mardi *m*   Tuesday
mars *m*   March
matin *m*   morning
mauvais   bad
meilleur   best
même   same, even
mer *f*   sea
merci (beaucoup)
       thank you (very much)

French-English Dictionary

mercredi *m* Wednesday
mère *f* mother
météo *f* weather report
métier *m* job
mettre to put, to place
meuble *m* furniture
midi *m* midday
mieux better
mince thin, slim
minuit *m* midnight
mode *f* fashion, method
moins (que) less (than)
mois *m* month
monnaie *f* change (money)
monsieur *m* Mr, sir
monter to go up, to get on
mot *m* word
moyen medium, average, way
mur *m* wall
musée *m* museum

N

nager to swim
ne ... aucun none, not one
ne ... pas not
ne ... personne
    no one, not anyone
ne ... plus no more, no longer
neige *f* snow
nettoyer to clean
neuf new
noir black
nord north
normalement normally
nouveau new
novembre *m* November
nuage *m* cloud
nuit *f* night
numéro *m* number

O

objets *mpl* trouvés lost property
occupé busy, occupied
octobre *m* October
oeil *m* / yeux *mpl* eye / eyes
office *m* de tourisme
    tourist office
ordinateur *m* computer
ou or
où where
oublier to forget
ouest west
ouvert open

P

par (ici) by, via (around here)
parce que because
parfois sometimes
parler to talk
partager to share
partir to leave
pas not
passer to pass, to sit (an exam)
passe-temps *m* pastimes
pays *m* country
pendant que while
perdre to lose
père *m* father
petit small
petit dèjeuner *m* breakfast
peu little, not much
peut-être maybe, perhaps
peux (I) can
plage *f* beach
plein full
pluie *f* rain
plus (que) more (than)
plusieurs several
porter to wear
pour for
pourquoi why
pouvoir can, to be able to
premier/première first
prendre to take
près de near, close
presque almost, nearly
prix *m* (fixe) (fixed) price
prochain next
proche near, close
puis then, next

Q

quand when
que that, which
quelque some
quelquefois sometimes
quelqu'un someone
qu'est-ce que what...?
qui who, which

R

raison *f* reason
ranger to tidy
remercier to thank
remplir to fill out
renseignements *mpl* information
repas *m* meal
rester to stay
résultat *m* result

retard – en retard late
réveiller to wake up
rez-de-chaussée *m* ground floor
rien nothing
rondpoint *m* roundabout
rouge red

S

salut hello, hi
samedi *m* Saturday
sans without
sauf except, apart from
savoir to know
se coucher to go to bed
semaine *f* week
septembre *m* September
sérieux serious
seulement only, just
si if
soeur *f* sister
soif – j'ai soif I'm thirsty
soir *m* evening
soldes *mpl* sale
sous-sol *m* basement
sud south
sur on
SVP – s'il vous plaît please
syndicat m d'initiative
    tourist office

T

tard late
temps *m* time, weather
terminer to finish
timbre *m* stamp
tomber to fall
toujours always
tout de suite straight away
traduire to translate
trop too much

U

utiliser to use

V

vendredi *m* Friday
venir (ici) to come (here)
vers towards, around
veux (I) want
vieux old
vite fast, quick
voici here is/are
vouloir to want

W, X, Y, X

y there

English-French Dictionary

A
able to   pouvoir
about   environ, vers
aeroplane   avion *m*
after(noon)   après(-midi) *m or f*
against   contre
agreed   d'accord
almost   presque
already   déjà
alright   ça va
also   aussi
always   toujours
and   et
apart from   sauf
arrive   arriver
as   comme
ask   demander
at   à

B
bad – awful   mauvais - affreux
badly   mal
basement   sous-sol *m*
be   être
beach   plage *f*
because   car, parce que
bed, bedroom   lit *m*, chambre *f*
before   avant, devant
behind   derrière
beside   à coté *m* de
best, better   meilleur, mieux
between   entre
bill   addition *f*
birthday   anniversaire *m*
black   noir
blue   bleu
boring   ennuyeux
bottle   bouteille *f*
box   boîte *f*
boy   garçon *m*
breakfast   petit dèjeuner *m*
brown   brun
building   bâtiment *m*
business   affaires *fpl*
but   mais
buy   acheter
by   de, en, par

C
can   pouvoir
change   changer
change (money)   monnaie *f*
chat   bavarder
choose   choisir
clean   nettoyer
close – near   près de, proche
closed   fermé
cloud   nuage *m*
coast   côte *f*

cold – I'm cold   froid - j'ai froid
colour   couleur *f*
come (here)   venir (ici)
computer   ordinateur *m*
cook   cuir
corner   coin *m*
country, countryside   pays *m*, campagne *f*
crossroads   carrefour *m*

D
dangerous   dangereux
daughter   fille *f*
day   jour *m*
dear, expensive   cher
decide   décider
delicious   délicieux
difficult   difficile, dur
dinner (evening meal)   dîner *m*
do   faire
drawing   dessin *m*
drink   boire

E
easy   facile
eat   manger
enjoyable   amusant
enough   assez
evening   soir *m*
exam   examen *m*
except   sauf
explain   expliquer

F
false – not true   faux
famous   célèbre
far from   loin de
fast   vite
fat   gros
finish   terminer
fire (fireworks)   feu *m* (feux d'artifice)
first, to begin with   d'abord
fog   brouillard *m*
food   alimentation *f*
for   depuis, pour
forbidden   interdit
forget   oublier
free, available   gratuit, libre
friend   ami(e)
from   de, depuis
full   complet, plein
funny   amusant

G
girl   fille *f*
give   donner
go – to bed   aller - se coucher
good   bon
good evening   bonsoir

good luck   bonne chance *f*
good morning/afternoon   bonjour
good night   bonne nuit
goodbye   au revoir
grey   gris
ground floor   rez-de-chaussée *m*

H
half   demi
happy   content, heureux
hard   dur
have, to have to   avoir, devoir
hear   entendre
heart   coeur *m*
hello, hi   salut
help, help!   aider, au secours!
homework   devoirs *mpl*
hope   espérer
hot   chaud
hour   heure *f*
house – my/your house   maison *f* – chez moi/toi
how, how much   comment, combien
hungry – I'm hungry   faim – j'ai faim

I
if   si
ill   malade
in   à, en, dans
included, inclusive   compris, inclus
into   en
invite   inviter
is...?   est-ce que
it   ça
it/this is   c'est
it/this was   c'était

J
job   emploi *m*, métier *m*

K
kind   gentil
know   connaître, savoir

L
language   langue *f*
large   gros
last   dernier
late   tard, en retard
learn   apprendre
least – at least   au moins
leave   partir
left   gauche
less (than)   moins (que)
like   aimer, comme
like (a lot)   adorer

English-French Dictionary

listen   écouter
little – not much   peu
live in   habiter
lose   perdre
lot – a lot   beaucoup
love   aimer
luck   chance f
lunch   déjeuner m

M

maybe   peut-être
meal   repas m
midday   midi m
midnight   minuit m
month   mois m
more (than)   encore, plus (que)
morning   matin m
much   beaucoup
museum   musée m

N

name   nom m
near   près de, proche
nearly   presque
need   avoir besoin de
never   jamais
new   nouveau, neuf
newspaper   journal m
next   prochain, puis, ensuite
nice   agréable, gentil, sympa
night   nuit f
noise   bruit m
not   ne ... pas
nothing   rien
now   maintenant

O

of   de
office   bureau m
OK   ça va, d'accord
on   en, sur
on foot   à pied
once   une fois
open   ouvert
opinion – in my opinion
    à mon avis m
opposite   contraire
or   ou
other   autre
outskirts   banlieue f

P

party   boum f
pastime   passe-temps m, loisir m
play   jouer
plate   assiette f
postcard   carte postale f
pound (sterling)   livre m (sterling)
present   cadeau m

price (fixed)   prix m (fixe)
pupil   élève m/f
put   mettre

Q

quick   vite

R

rain   pluie f
read   lire
reason   raison f
red   rouge
right – correct   droite – vrai
roughly   environ

S

same   même
say   dire
sea, seaside
    mer f, bord m de la mer
seat   siège m, place f
second   deuxième
send   envoyer
serious   sérieux
several   plusieurs
share   partager
shower   douche f
side, way   côté m
since – as   depuis – car
sing / song   chanter / chanson f
size   taille f, pointure f
sleep   dormir
slowly   lentement
small   petit
snow   neige f
so   alors, donc
some   quelque
someone   quelqu'un
sometimes   parfois, quelquefois
son   fils m
sorry   désolé
stay   rester
strong   fort
study   étudier

T

take   prendre
talk   parler
thank you (very much)
    merci (beaucoup)
that   ça, que
the   le / la / les / l'
then   alors, ensuite, puis
there   là, là-bas, y
there is, there are   il y a
there isn't/aren't   il n'y a pas
there will be/were   il y aura/avait
therefore   donc
thin   mince

thing   chose f
thirsty – I'm thirsty
    soif – j'ai soif
this one, that one   ceci, cela
this, these   ce, cet, etc.
ticket, ticket office
    billet m, guichet m
tidy   ranger
time   temps m, fois f
timetable   horaire m
tired   fatigué
to   à, dans
today   aujourd'hui
tomorrow   demain
tooth brush   brosse à dents f
towards   vers
translate   traduire
try   essayer

U

understand
    comprendre, connaître
until   jusqu'à
use   utiliser
usually   d'habitude

V

vacuum cleaner   aspirateur m

W

wait   attendre
wall   mur m
want   vouloir
wash   laver
wear   porter
weather – report
    temps – météo m
week   semaine f
welcome   bienvenue
well   bien, alors
what   qu'est-ce que
when   quand
where   où
which   que, qui
while   pendant que
white   blanc
who   qui
why   pourquoi
wife   femme f
with   avec
without   sans
write   écrire

X, Y, Z

year   an m, année f
yellow   jaune
yesterday   hier
yet   encore
young   jeune

Index

If the word you want isn't here, then look up the topic heading it would come under — so, if you want *swimming* look up *sport*, or if you want to find *eggs* then look up *food*.

Index

FHR40